剑桥KET考试
写作通关周计划

金利 / 编著

化学工业出版社
·北京·

图书在版编目（CIP）数据

剑桥KET考试写作通关周计划 / 金利编著 . —北京：
化学工业出版社，2024.4
（剑桥KET考试通关周计划）
ISBN 978-7-122-45249-8

Ⅰ.①剑…　Ⅱ.①金…　Ⅲ.①英语水平考试-写作-
自学参考资料　Ⅳ.①H315

中国国家版本馆CIP数据核字（2024）第055500号

责任编辑：马小桐　马　骄　加工编辑：温建斌　装帧设计：张　辉
责任校对：杜杏然　　　　　　　　　　　　　版式设计：梧桐影

出版发行：化学工业出版社
　　　　　（北京市东城区青年湖南街13号　邮政编码100011）
印　　装：河北京平诚乾印刷有限公司
787mm×1092mm　1/16　印张10　字数177千字
2024年6月北京第1版第1次印刷

购书咨询：010-64518888　　　　　售后服务：010-64518899
网　　址：http://www.cip.com.cn
凡购买本书，如有缺损质量问题，本社销售中心负责调换。

定　　价：49.90元　　　　　　　　　版权所有　违者必究

前言

　　《剑桥KET考试写作通关周计划》一书写给正在备考剑桥A2 Key(KET)写作考试的考生。我们深知准备写作考试需要一定的时间规划、思路点拨、考点锦囊以及充分练习。因此，本书采用讲解与规划相结合的学习方法，将这些要素有机地结合在一起，帮助考生顺利通关。

　　🕐 KET考试写作通关 = **合理的时间规划 + 思路点拨 + 考点锦囊 + 每周一练**

★ 8周学习规划

　　按周规划好学习内容，跟着规划学，易坚持，更高效。

　　本书学习内容以周为单位，从考试内容入手，为考生规划好要学习和练习的内容，跟着规划走，利用碎片化时间来学习，用时少，效率高。

　　◇【周目标】每周开启学习前，了解本周学习目标。

　　◇【周中学】每周周中学习考试核心备考知识，掌握答题思路，积累考试词句。

　　◇【周末练】周六周日，集中演练本周所学。

　　一周内容，以目标为导向，学练结合，知识掌握更加扎实。

★ 思路点拨 + 考点锦囊

　　考题呈现，剖析答题思路，分享KET写作锦囊，答题更容易。

　　在每周学习中，针对写作考试中的题型，本书给出了答题思路以及考点锦囊。同时，本书还包含KET写作Part 6和Part 7考试的常考话题，并给出与话题相关的句型和答题关键点，为考生提供写作的资料库。

本书旨在帮助考生建立答题思维，而非死记硬背，有思路，有方法，有词句积累，考场答题更从容。

★ 每周一练+全真模拟

多样化题型操练本周所学，学后巩固练习，知识掌握更加扎实。

本书的练习题包括各种多样化的写作题型，如选词填空、圈出正确的单词、连线、判断句子正误、改写句子、组词成句等，内容涉及动词过去式、时间介词、常用形容词、副词、连词等多项写作语法知识点，多维度操练所学内容，进一步夯实所学，打好基础，帮助考生有效备考。

通过每周一练和全真模拟题，考生将能够熟悉各种考试题型，提高写作能力，并在实践中提高应对考试的信心。

总之，本书致力于为考生提供全面而高效的学习资源，让考生在备考剑桥A2 Key(KET)写作考试时更有信心、更具备竞争力。希望通过本书的学习，考生能够顺利通过考试，实现自己的考试目标。

目录

Week

7

看图作文：假期游玩

Week

8

考试全流程模拟练习

熟悉考试

第1周目标

考试模块	时间	主题	
写作	Day 1	了解考试题型及要求	☐
	Day 2	答题卡填写注意事项	☐
	Day 3	熟悉评分标准	☐
	Day 4	熟悉常考话题	☐
	Day 5	写作必备技能	☐
	Weekend	每周一练	☐

Day 1　了解考试题型及要求

A2 Key写作共有两个部分：阅读和写作（Reading and Writing）试卷的Part 6和Part 7。官方建议写作部分的答题时间为20分钟。Part 6为邮件写作，Part 7为看图作文。Part 6的写作词数要求是不少于25个词，Part 7的写作词数要求是不少于35个词。

部分	任务	要求	题数	分数
Part 6	邮件写作	根据所给信息写一篇邮件或便条，作文长度不少于25个词	1	15
Part 7	看图作文	根据所给的三张图片，写一篇不少于35个词的小故事	1	15

任务	考查能力
邮件写作	从内容、组织结构、语言能力三个方面，考查考生能否写出具有交际目的的短文的能力
看图作文	从内容、组织结构和语言能力三个方面，考查考生能否根据三张图片写出一个完整的短故事的能力

下面是写作部分的官方备考建议。

Part 6 官方建议	
1	考生应仔细阅读考试说明
2	考生需要确定题目规定的作文是什么类型，以及写作对象是谁
3	考生应考虑作文中需要包含哪些信息
4	考生须对题目中所给的三个提示做出应答
5	考生应先在草稿纸上打个草稿，然后再在答题卡上写下最终答案

Part 7 官方建议	
1	考生应仔细阅读考试说明
2	考生需要观察图片，然后找出故事中包含的三个主要事件
3	考生应考虑文章中需要包含哪些信息
4	考生须提及三张图片中涉及的所有提示
5	考生应先在草稿纸上打个草稿，然后再在答题卡上写下最终答案

Day 2　答题卡填写注意事项

下面是A2 Key写作部分试卷答题卡具体填写要求以及注意事项。

1. A2 Key写作部分答题均用铅笔完成。

2. 答题卡要使用B/HB铅笔填涂。

3. 确认答案后将对应圆圈涂满、涂黑。

4. 字迹清晰，卷面整洁。

1. 考卷上已有信息，无须填写，只须核对

Draft

OFFICE USE ONLY - DO NOT WRITE OR MAKE ANY MARK ABOVE THIS LINE   Page 1 of 2

Cambridge Assessment
English

Candidate Name

Centre Name

Examination Title

Candidate Signature

Candidate Number

Centre Number

Examination Details

Assessment Date

Supervisor: If the candidate is ABSENT or has WITHDRAWN shade here ○

3. 缺考标记，考生勿填

2. 上面信息核对无误后，在此处填姓名拼音（大写），如 LI HUA

Key for Schools Writing

Candidate Answer Sheet for Parts 6 and 7

INSTRUCTIONS TO CANDIDATES

Make sure that your name and candidate number are on this sheet.

Write your answers to Writing Parts 6 and 7 on the other side of this sheet.

Use a pencil.

You **must** write within the grey lines.

Do **not** write on the bar codes.

OFFICE USE ONLY - DO NOT WRITE OR MAKE ANY MARK BELOW THIS LINE   Page 1 of 2

Draft

Draft

4. A2 Key 是铅笔作答，要求字迹清晰，卷面整洁

Part 6: Write your answer below.

Part 7: Write your answer below.

Examiner's Use Only

Part 6	C	O	L		Part 7	C	O	L

5. 考官填写区，
考生勿填

Draft

Day 3 | 熟悉评分标准

A2 Key写作考试的评分标准共有三项：内容、组织结构、语言能力。

具体的评分标准如下。

得分档	内容	组织结构	语言能力
5	◆ 所有内容紧扣题目 ◆ 目标读者可以理解全部内容	◆ 文章联系紧密，条理清晰，能运用基础的连接词和个别衔接方式	◆ 日常词汇运用得当，偶尔重复使用某些词汇 ◆ 可以做到熟练使用简单的语法形式 ◆ 虽然有错误，但不影响理解
4	写作水平介于5分档和3分档之间		
3	◆ 内容稍微有些跑题或要点不全 ◆ 目标读者基本可以理解所写内容	◆ 文章联系紧密，能使用基础的高频连接词	◆ 可以合理、恰当地使用基础词汇 ◆ 会使用一些简单的语法形式 ◆ 有时会犯一些妨碍读者理解的错误
2	写作水平介于3分档和1分档之间		
1	◆ 内容跑题，题目解读错误 ◆ 目标读者很难理解所写内容	◆ 文章联系不紧密，但偶尔会使用标点符号和and这种简单的连接词	◆ 能够写出个别单词和短语 ◆ 基本不会使用简单的语法形式
0	◆ 内容完全跑题 ◆ 目标读者无法理解所写内容	写作水平低于1分档	

从上述评分标准中可以看出，要想写作部分得高分，须做到以下几点。

1. 写作时，要涵盖题目中给出的所有要点。（Part 6的3个问题；Part 7的3幅图片）

2. 写作长度达到词数要求。（Part 6词数≥25；Part 7词数≥35）

3. 语言得体恰当，语法正确，句意明确。（详情见"Day 5写作必备技能"）

4. 文章联系紧密，条理清晰，能运用基础的连接词和个别衔接方式。（详情见"Day 5 写作必备技能"）

Day 4　熟悉常考话题

一、Part 6常考话题

A2 Key Part 6写作考的是考生熟悉的话题，共分8类，分别为休闲爱好、日常生活、假期旅行、体育运动、学校、购物、食物和健康，其中包括的内容有个人信息、博物馆、音乐会、电影、生日、露营、比赛等。

序号	常考话题	内容	篇数	占比
1	休闲爱好	博物馆之旅	4	26%
		音乐会		
		最喜欢的电影		
		相约去动物园		
2	日常生活	个人信息	3	20%
		生日礼物		
		笔记本		
3	假期旅行	假期旅行	2	13%
		无法去露营		
4	体育运动	自行车比赛	2	13%
		借篮球		
5	学校	新学校	1	7%
6	购物	购物	1	7%
7	食物	特别喜欢的食物	1	7%
8	健康	生病	1	7%

二、Part 6邮件类型

A2 Key Part 6是邮件/便条写作，邮件/便条类型有9类，分别为介绍类、计划类、经历类、推荐类、邀请类、道歉类、感谢类、求助类、请假类。

序号	邮件类型	内容	答题要点
1	介绍类	介绍一般事实或将来的某种情况	熟练使用现在时

序号	邮件类型	内容	答题要点
2	计划类	介绍将来的某种计划	熟练使用将来时
3	经历类	回复对方的询问，介绍过去发生的事情	熟练使用过去时，尤其是动词的过去式
4	推荐类	介绍或推荐书籍、电影等	熟悉常见的喜好表达等
5	邀请类	邀请对方参加聚会、游玩等	熟悉邀请类的常用表达
6	道歉类	告知对方无法赴约等	熟悉表示歉意的常用表达
7	感谢类	感谢对方给的礼物、帮助等	熟练掌握表达感谢的常见句型
8	求助类	请求帮助或借东西等	熟练掌握请求帮助的委婉表达
9	请假类	请假休息等	熟练掌握请假的委婉表达
*详情见"Day 5写作必备技能"			

三、Part 7常考话题

A2 Key Part 7写作考的是考生熟悉的话题，主要分3大类，分别为日常生活、休闲活动和假期游玩。其中内容多为生活中的经历，比如"开学前一天""整理卧室"等；生活中的趣事，比如"梦中吹气球""购物小帮手"等；生活中的惊喜，比如"生日惊喜"等；生活中的意外，比如"猫打碎花瓶"等。

序号	常考话题	内容	篇数	占比
1	日常生活	开学前一天	5	33.33%
		整理卧室		
		梦中吹气球		
		猫打碎花瓶		
		邻里互助		
2	休闲活动	跑步比赛	5	33.33%
		放风筝		
		画画乐事		
		购物小帮手		
		生日惊喜		

续表

序号	常考话题	内容	篇数	占比
3	假期游玩	动物园之旅	5	33.33%
		海边度假		
		班级旅行		
		雨后出游		
		公园游玩		

Day 5　写作必备技能

一、写作常用的五种时态

　　A2 Key写作常用的五种时态：一般现在时、一般过去时、一般将来时、过去进行时、现在完成时。

常用时态	举例	用法
一般现在时	It **is** a very beautiful city. 这是一个非常美丽的城市。	◆ 描述习惯、兴趣和日常行为 ◆ 描述客观事实 ◆ 表达观点
一般过去时	I **watched** TV last night. 我昨晚看电视了。	◆ 描述过去发生的事
一般将来时	I **am going to** visit my grandma tomorrow. 我明天要去看望我的奶奶。 We **will** ride to the park. 我们将骑车去公园。	◆ 讲述未来的计划
过去进行时	Jack **was walking** home from school. 杰克正从学校走回家。	◆ 描述过去正在发生的事
现在完成时	The movie which I **have seen** twice is *The Wandering Earth*. 我看过两遍的电影是《流浪地球》。	◆ 描述过去的事对现在有影响

　　下面是A2 Key写作中常用的一般过去时和一般将来时的标志词。

常用时态	常用词	举例	
一般过去时	last +...	yesterday 昨天	the day before yesterday 前天
		last night 昨晚	**last** month 上个月
		last week 上周	**last** Sunday 上周日

常用时态	常用词	举例	
一般过去时	...+ ago	three days **ago** 三天前	
	其他	one day 一天 at that time 在那时	once upon a time 从前
一般将来时		tomorrow 明天 this evening 今天晚上	today 今天
	next +...	**next** week 下周	**next** Sunday 下周日
	in +	**in** a week's time 一周后 **in** the future 在未来	**in** two months' time 两个月后
	其他	some day 总有一天 later on 稍后	soon 不久之后

二、写作常用连接词

A2 Key写作考试中，使用连接词是提升作文质量的有效方法之一。通过使用连接词，考生可以将简单句转化为长句，从而增加句子的复杂性和表达的丰富性。常见的连接词有八类：

◆ 表并列：and、or

◆ 表因果：because、so（*because和so不能同时使用）

◆ 表转折：but、although（*although和but不能同时使用）、however

◆ 表递进：especially、besides

◆ 表举例：like、such as、for example

◆ 引导从句：that、who、which

◆ 表时间顺序：when、while、after

◆ 表条件：if

考生在使用连接词时需要注意理清两个简单句之间的逻辑关系，确保句子之间的衔接自然、流畅。通过合理使用连接词，考生的作文将更容易脱颖而出，并获得更高的分数。

序号	连接词		举例
1	表并列	and 和	He looked on their computer **and** quickly found a restaurant. 他在电脑上看了看，很快就找到了一家餐馆。
		or 或者	We can go to the cinema on Saturday **or** Sunday. 我们可以在星期六或星期天去看电影。

序号		连接词	举例
2	表因果	because 因为	She wants to buy a gift for her dad **because** his birthday is coming soon. 她想给爸爸买一份礼物，因为爸爸的生日快到了。
		so 所以	He got up late in the morning, **so** he missed the bus. 他早上起晚了，所以没赶上公交车。
3	表转折	but 但是	They arrived at the cinema, **but** the door was closed. 他们到了电影院，但门却关着。
		although 虽然，尽管	**Although** the sun was shining it wasn't very warm. 虽然阳光灿烂，但并不很暖和。
		however 然而	**However**, her bike broke down halfway, and there was no place to repair it. 然而，她的自行车中途坏了，还没有地方修理。
4	表递进	especially 尤其，特别	She loves all sports, **especially** swimming. 她喜爱各种运动，尤其是游泳。
		Besides 除……之外	We have lots of things in common **besides** music. 除了音乐，我们还有很多共通点。
5	表举例	like 例如	I like to read books, **like** *Harry Potter* and *The Lord of the Rings*. 我喜欢阅读书籍，例如《哈利·波特》和《指环王》。
		such as 比如	We'll do many things **such as** eating, playing sports, and chatting. 我们会做很多事情，比如吃饭、运动和聊天。
		for example 例如	**For example**, we can go to the movies on Saturday. 例如，我们可以在星期六去看电影。
6	引导从句	that 作关系代词	It's the best novel (**that**) I've ever read. 这是我读过的最棒的小说。
		who 表示所指的人	I saw a man in the street **who** is playing the guitar. 我在街上看见一个正在弹吉他的人。
		which 表示所指的物	The old man is carrying a bag **which** looks heavy. 老人提着一个看起来很重的包。
7	表时间顺序	when 当……时候	**When** she arrived at the park, she met one of her classmates. 当她到达公园时，她遇到了她的一个同学。
		while 当……的时候	**While** Lily was walking, she picked up a bag on the road. 当莉莉走路的时候，她在路上捡到了一个包。
		after 在……以后	**After** an hour I went home. 一小时之后我回家了。
8	表条件	if 如果	**If** it rains tomorrow, we'll stay at home. 如果明天下雨，我们就待在家里。

Weekend 二 每周一练

为帮助考生快速熟悉考题，我们摘录了A2 Key写作官方样题、考生作文、考官评分及点评，并在每篇点评后面附上了中文翻译和知识点详解。

Part 6 官方样题

Question 31

You are going shopping with your English friend Pat tomorrow.
Write an email to Pat.

Say:

- where you want to meet
- what time you want to meet
- what you want to buy

Write **25 words** or more.
Write the email on your answer sheet.

Part 6 考生作文和考官评分及点评

Candidate A

Hi Pat,

I am so happy to going shopping with you tomorrow because I want to buy new football boots. We can meet at your house at 11:00. Is it OK for you? Then we take a bus.

See you tomorrow.

 Commentary and mark

Very good attempt at the task. The content of the message is relevant to the task and all three elements of the message are clearly communicated. The text is coherent and basic linking words and cohesive devices (because, then, it) are used. Everyday vocabulary is used appropriately and even though there are some errors with the grammatical forms used, the meaning is still completely clear.

写作任务完成得非常好。作文内容与题目相关，且题目中给出的3个信息要点作文中均已清晰阐述。作文连贯，使用了基础的连接词和衔接技巧（because、then、it）。日常词汇运用得当。尽管语法形式上有一些错误，但不影响句意理解。

修改

I am so happy to **going** shopping with you tomorrow because I want to buy new football boots.

I am so happy to go shopping with you tomorrow because I want to buy new football boots.

*知识点：I am so happy to do sth. 我很高兴做某事。

评分

| 内容：5 | 组织结构：5 | 语言能力：5 | 总分：15 |

Candidate B

I'm really happy to go to shopping tomorrow. Let's meet in a coffee in a shopping centre and I want to buy my present of my brother.

 Commentary and mark

Satisfactory attempt at the task. The target reader is informed about bullet point 1 and 3, but the time to meet is missing from the message. The text is coherent, and punctuation and the simple linking word "and" are used to help organize the text. Some simple grammatical forms are used with some control. The errors in the second sentence (Let's meet in a coffee) and in the third sentence (I want to buy my present of my brother) may make it difficult to understand the meaning at times.

本次写作任务完成得还可以。目标读者能了解要点1和要点3的信息，但作文中漏掉了"见面时间"这个要点。行文连贯，使用了标点符号和简单的连接词and。会用一些简单的语法形式。第2句（Let's meet in a coffee... I want to buy my present of my brother）中的错误可能会妨碍读者理解句意。

修改

I'm really happy to **go to shopping** tomorrow.

I'm really happy to go shopping tomorrow.

*知识点：go shopping是固定词组，意为"去购物"。

Let's meet **in a coffee** in a shopping centre and I want to **buy** my present **of** my brother.

Let's meet **at the cafe** in the shopping centre. I want to **buy** a birthday present **for** my brother.

*知识点：①coffee意为"咖啡"，表示"在咖啡馆"用at the cafe；

②buy sb. sth.或buy sth. for sb. 意为"给某人买某物"，

比如buy me a new coat = buy a new coat for me 给我买一件新外套。

 评分

内容：3	组织结构：3	语言能力：3	总分：9

Part 7 官方样题

Question 32

Look at the three pictures.

Write the story shown in the pictures.

Write **35 words** or more.

Write the story on your answer sheet.

Part 7 考生作文和考官评分及点评

Candidate A

Last Saturday I went to a picnic with my friends. First, we put the fruits, sandwich and orange juice in my bag, then we went. When we arrived at the camping, we ate on the floor, then Tom and Lucy went to the lake and Michel and I saw them.

 Commentary and mark

Very good attempt at the task. All of the content of the story is relevant to the task and the connections between the pictures are clearly shown using basic linking words and cohesive devices (and, first, then, when, we), so the reader can fully understand the story. Vocabulary is generally used appropriately, and even though there are some small errors with the grammatical forms used, the meaning is still clear.

本次写作任务完成得非常好。作文中的所有内容都与题目相关，并且通过使用基础的连接词和衔接方式（and、first、then、when、we），清楚地体现了图片之间的联系，读者可以充分理解故事内容。文中词汇的使用基本得当，尽管语法形式上有一些小错误，但意思还是清楚的。

修改

Last Saturday I **went to a picnic** with my friends.

⬇

Last Saturday I went for a picnic with my friends.

*知识点：go for a picnic是固定搭配，意为"去野餐"。

First, we put the fruits, **sandwich** and orange juice in my bag, then we **went**.

⬇

First, we put the fruits, sandwiches and orange juice in my bag, then we went out.

*知识点：①sandwich意为"三明治"为可数名词，复数形式为sandwiches；

②表示"出门"用go out。

When we arrived at the **camping**, we ate on the floor, then Tom and Lucy **went to the lake** and Michel and I saw them.

⬇

When we arrived at the camping site, we ate on the floor, then Tom and Lucy went for a swim in the lake and Michel and I saw them.

*知识点：①表示"露营地"用camping site；

②表"去湖里游泳"用"go for a swim in the lake"或"go swimming in the lake"。

评分

内容：5	组织结构：5	语言能力：5	总分：15

Candidate B

Four people went to a picnic and they sit by a lake. They ate food and drank drinks. Two of people are kids. Kids going to swim so parents was sawing their kids. Then they went to home.

Commentary and mark

Satisfactory attempt at task. Although the first picture is not mentioned in the text, the rest of the story is mainly communicated clearly. The reader is on the whole informed. The text is connected using basic linking words (and, so). The candidate has used the correct verbs and some basic relevant vocabulary (sit by a lake, food, kids, swim), and some simple grammatical forms are used with some degree of control.

本次写作任务完成得还可以。虽然作文中没有提及第1张图片中的内容，但后两张图片中的故事要点基本上表达清楚了。读者大体上能理解故事内容。作文中使用了一些基础的连接词（and、so）。考生可以正确使用动词以及一些基础的相关词汇（sit by a lake、food、kids、swim），也能比较自如地使用一些简单的语法形式。

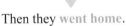

Four people **went to a picnic** and they **sit** by a lake.

Four people went for a picnic and they sat by a lake.

*知识点：①go for a picnic为固定词组，意为"去野餐"；

②sit意为"坐"，过去式为sat。

Kids **going** to swim so parents was **sawing** their kids.

Kids went swimming so parents were looking at their kids.

*知识点：①go swimming为固定搭配，意为"去游泳"；

②see不用于进行时，表示"看着"可用look at。

Then they **went to home**.

Then they went home.

*知识点：go home为固定词组，意为"回家"。

| 内容：3 | 组织结构：3 | 语言能力：3 | 总分：9 |

Week 2 邮件写作：介绍一般事实、未来计划

第2周目标

考试模块	时间	主题	内容	
Part 6 邮件写作	Day 1	介绍：个人信息	I'm glad to receive your message.	☐
	Day 2	介绍：新学校	My new school is located in ...	☐
	Day 3	计划：购物	I'm writing to you about my shopping plan ...	☐
	Day 4	计划：博物馆之旅	Looking forward to our trip to ...	☐
	Day 5	请假：生病	May I kindly request a day off tomorrow?	☐
	Weekend	每周一练	基础练习	☐

Day 1　介绍：个人信息

 考场模拟

Read this note from your penfriend, Amy.

> Hi, Lucy.
>
> I'm Amy, your new penfriend. How old are you? Do you have any brothers and sisters? What is your favourite hobby?

Write a note to Amy. Answer the questions.

Write **25 words** or more.

 思路点拨

Step 1:【审题，划重点】

弄清楚以下三点：

- 便条写给谁
- 写便条的原因

● 要回答的三个问题

Read this note from your penfriend, Amy. —— 要给她写便条

Hi, Lucy.

I'm Amy, your new penfriend.

- **How old** are you?
- Do you **have any brothers and sisters?**　} 要回答的3个问题
- What is **your favourite hobby**?

Write a note to Amy. Answer the questions. —— 写便条的目的

Step 2:【回答三个问题】

	how old 多大	11 years old 11岁
		I am ... 我……
回答问题	brothers or sisters 兄弟姐妹	a seven-year-old sister 一个七岁的妹妹
		I have ... 我有……
	favourite hobby 最喜欢的爱好	play the violin 拉小提琴
		I usually ... 我通常……

Step 3:【组句成段】

1. 表明回复目的：I'm glad to ...

2. 回答三个问题

3. 结尾语：Best wishes,

Step 4:【检查修改】

□ 1. 开头称呼和结束语正确　　　□ 2. 回答了3个问题

□ 3. 词数≥25　　　　　　　　　□ 4. 无拼写错误

□ 5. 无语法错误

高分范文

Dear Amy,

I am glad to receive your message. I am eleven years old. I have a seven-year-old sister. I usually play the violin in my spare time. Hope we can meet soon!

Best wishes,

Lucy

（词数：36）

参考译文

亲爱的艾米：

很高兴收到你的信息。我今年十一岁。我有一个七岁的妹妹。我通常在业余时间拉小提琴。希望我们能尽快见面！

祝好

露西

 考点锦囊

类似seven-year-old的用法		
☑	☒	用法
a three-month-old baby 一个三个月的婴儿	× a three month old baby	复合形容词中，单词与单词之间要有连字符
a two-week school trip 一次两个礼拜的学校旅行	× a two-weeks school trip	复合形容词中的名词只能用单数，不能用复数

"基数词"相关表达		
1～10	11～19	20～100
one 1	eleven 11	twen**ty** 20
two 2	twelve 12	thir**ty** 30
three 3	thir**teen** 13	for**ty** 40
four 4	four**teen** 14	fif**ty** 50
five 5	fif**teen** 15	six**ty** 60
six 6	six**teen** 16	seven**ty** 70
seven 7	seven**teen** 17	eigh**ty** 80
eight 8	eigh**teen** 18	nine**ty** 90
nine 9	nine**teen** 19	hundred 100
ten 10		

*回答年龄，用**基数词**，有两种表达方式：
①I'm + 基数词，比如：I'm **eleven**. 我今年11岁。
②I'm + 基数词 + years old，比如：I'm **eleven** years old. 我今年11岁。

"序数词"相关表达		
第1~10	第11~19	第20~100
first 第1	eleven**th** 第11	twentie**th** 第20
second 第2	twelf**th** 第12	thirtie**th** 第30
third 第3	thirteen**th** 第13	fortie**th** 第40
fourth 第4	fourteen**th** 第14	fiftie**th** 第50
fifth 第5	fifteen**th** 第15	sixtie**th** 第60
sixth 第6	sixteen**th** 第16	seventie**th** 第70
seventh 第7	seventeen**th** 第17	eightie**th** 第80
eighth 第8	eighteen**th** 第18	ninetie**th** 第90
ninth 第9	nineteen**th** 第19	hundred**th** 第100
tenth 第10		
*序数词用来表示顺序，与定冠词the连用，表示"第几"，比如the first（第一）、the second（第二）		

"家人朋友"相关表达		
dad 爸爸	parents 父母	daughter 女儿
father 父亲	grandma 奶奶；外婆	son 儿子
mum 妈妈	grandpa 爷爷；外公	cousin 堂兄弟；堂姐妹
mother 母亲	aunt 伯母；姨母	penfriend 笔友
brother 哥哥；弟弟	uncle 舅父；伯父	friend 朋友
sister 姐姐；妹妹		

"兴趣爱好"相关表达		
piano 钢琴	singing 唱歌	swimming 游泳
violin 小提琴	dancing 跳舞	fishing 钓鱼
guitar 吉他	painting 画画	gardening 园艺
cello 大提琴	reading 读书	running 跑步
stamp collecting 集邮	cooking 烹饪	photography 摄影
horse-riding 骑马		
*表示乐器的名词前加the，比如：play the piano 弹钢琴		

★ *必会句型* ★

1. 收到来信很高兴

I am glad to receive your message. 很高兴收到你的信息。

2. 自己年龄

I am ... years old. 我今年……岁。

3. 家人及年龄

1) I have a five-year-old brother. 我有一个5岁的弟弟。

2) I have one older brother. 我有一个哥哥。

4. 兴趣爱好

1) I usually ... in my spare time. 我通常在业余时间……

2) My favourite hobby is reading. 我最大的爱好是读书。

5. 期待见面

Hope we can meet soon! 希望我们能尽快见面!

Day 2　介绍：新学校

 考场模拟

You are studying in a new school now.

Write an email to your friend Casey about the school.

In your email:

- tell Casey where your school is

- say which teacher you like best and why

Write **25 words** or more.

 思路点拨

Step 1:【审题，划重点】

弄清楚以下三点：

- 邮件写给谁

- 写邮件的原因
- 要回答的三个问题

You are studying in a new school now. —————— 要给她写邮件

Write an email to your friend **Casey** about the school. ————— 写邮件的目的

In your email:

- tell Casey **where** your school is
- say **which teacher** you like best and **why**

} 要回答的3个问题

Step 2:【回答三个问题】

回答问题	where 哪里	downtown area 市中心
		I wanted to tell you that my new school is located ... 我想告诉你，我的新学校位于……
	which teacher 哪位老师	Ms. Johnson 约翰逊老师
		Oh, and I have a favourite teacher ...
	why 为什么	fun 有趣 think outside the box 跳出思维定式
		She makes learning fun and always encourages us to ... 她让学习变得有趣，并总是鼓励我们……

Step 3:【组句成段】

1. 表明写信目的：I hope this email finds you well. I wanted to tell you ...

2. 回答三个问题

3. 结尾语：Best wishes,

Step 4:【检查修改】

☐ 1. 开头称呼和结束语正确   ☐ 2. 回答了3个问题

☐ 3. 词数≥25   ☐ 4. 无拼写错误

☐ 5. 无语法错误

📄 高分范文

Hey Casey,

I hope this email finds you well. I wanted to tell you that my new school is located in the downtown area. It's quite convenient! I have a favourite teacher here—Ms. Johnson. She makes learning fun and always encourages us to think outside the box.

Best wishes,

Jim

（词数：51）

参考译文

嘿，凯西：

我希望你收到这封信时一切都好。我想告诉你，我的新学校位于市中心，很方便！在这儿我有一位最喜欢的老师——约翰逊老师。她让学习变得有趣，并总是鼓励我们跳出思维定式。

祝好

吉姆

 考点锦囊

"地理位置" 相关表达	
in the city centre 在市中心	near the park 在公园附近
in the downtown area 在市区	near the train station 靠近火车站
in the heart of the city 在城市的中心地带	near the bus stop 靠近公交车站
in the countryside 在乡村	next to the hospital 在医院旁边
in a coastal area 在海岸地区	on a main road 在一条主要道路上
in a quiet neighbourhood 在安静的社区里	in the suburbs 在郊区
in a residential area 在居民区	on the outskirts 在市郊
on the outskirts of the town 在城镇的郊外	across from the library 在图书馆对面
close to the highway 靠近高速公路	along the river 沿着河边
close to the shopping mall 靠近购物中心	by the river 在河边

喜欢某位老师的原因	
fun 有趣的	friendly 友好的
interesting 有趣的	humorous 幽默的

续表

喜欢某位老师的原因	
patient 耐心的	caring 体贴人的
supportive 给予帮助的	knowledgeable 博学的
encouraging 鼓励人的	teach well 教得好
make the class interesting 让课堂有趣	make learning enjoyable 让学习充满乐趣
fun activities and games 有趣的活动和游戏	give me praise 给予我赞美
show care and kindness 表现出关心和善良	explain things clearly 把事情解释得很清楚

★必会句型★

1. 写信开头的问候语

1) How is everything? 一切都好吗?

2) I hope you're doing well! 希望你一切安好!

3) I hope this email finds you well. 希望你收到此信时一切安好。

4) I hope you are doing great. 希望你一切都好。

5) I hope everything is going well with you. 希望你一切都好。

6) I hope everything is all right. 希望你一切都好。

2. 介绍新学校

I wanted to tell you that my new school ... 我想告诉你, 我的新学校……

3. 地理位置

It's located in the heart of the city, just a few blocks away from the central park. 它位于市中心, 离中央公园只有几个街区。

4. 最喜欢的老师

I have met some amazing teachers here, but my favourite is Miss Brighton. 我在这里遇到了一些很棒的老师, 但我最喜欢的是布莱顿老师。

5. 喜欢这位老师的原因

1) She teaches English and her classes are always so engaging and fun. 她教英语, 她的课总是那么迷人和有趣。

2) She has a great sense of humour and knows how to make learning enjoyable. 她很有幽默感, 知道如何使学习变得愉快。

Day 3　　计划：购物

考场模拟

You want to go shopping with your friend Amy this Saturday. Write an email to Amy.

Say:

- where you want to meet
- when you want to meet
- what you want to buy

Write **25 words** or more.

思路点拨

Step 1:【审题，划重点】

弄清楚以下三点：

- 邮件写给谁
- 写邮件的原因
- 要回答的三个问题

写邮件的目的　　　　　　　　　　　　　　要给她写邮件

You want to **go shopping** with your friend Amy **this Saturday**. Write an email to **Amy**.

Say:

- **where** you want to meet
- **when** you want to meet　　　　要回答的3个问题
- **what** you want to **buy**

Step 2:【回答三个问题】

	where 哪里	at the department store 在百货公司
回答问题		We can meet ... 我们可以见面……
	when 什么时候	10 o'clock 十点钟
		How / What about meeting at ...? 在……见面如何？

续表

| 回答问题 | what to buy
买什么 | T-shirt T恤 |
| | | I'd like to buy ... 我想要买…… |

Step 3:【组句成段】

1. 表明写信目的：I'm writing to ...

2. 回答三个问题

3. 结尾语：See you soon.

Step 4:【检查修改】

☐ 1. 开头称呼和结束语正确 ☐ 2. 回答了3个问题

☐ 3. 词数≥25 ☐ 4. 无拼写错误

☐ 5. 无语法错误

高分范文

Hi Amy,

I'm writing to you about my shopping plan this Saturday. I'd like to buy a new T-shirt. Would you like to come with me? We can meet at the department store. How about meeting at 10 o'clock?

See you soon.

Helen

（词数：43）

参考译文

嗨，艾米：

我写信给你是关于我本周六的购物计划。我想买一件新T恤。你愿意和我一起去吗？我们可以在百货商店见面。十点见面怎么样？

到时见。

海伦

 ## 考点锦囊

"见面地点" 相关表达	
at my house 在我家	at the department store 在百货商场

续表

"见面地点" 相关表达	
at the ticket house 在售票处	in the shopping centre 在购物中心
at the subway station 在地铁站	in the park 在公园
at the bus station 在公交车站	at the cinema 在电影院

"城市地点" 相关表达		
bookshop 书店	museum 博物馆	bus stop 公交站
theatre 剧院	zoo 动物园	pet shop 宠物店
gym 体育馆	park 公园	square 广场
sports centre 体育中心	cinema 电影院	bank 银行
restaurant 餐馆	shopping centre 购物中心	chemist 药店
cafe 咖啡馆	department store 百货商店	post office 邮局
cafeteria 食堂	supermarket 超市	

"时间" 相关表达	
分类	举例
整点	9:00 = nine o'clock
30分钟以内	10:06 = ten past six
半点	11:30 = half past eleven
30分钟以后	8:45 = a quarter to nine = fifteen to nine
a.m. 上午	8 a.m. 上午8点
p.m. 下午	2 p.m. 下午2点
*在具体的时刻前用介词at，比如at ten o'clock 在10点	

"购买的东西" 相关表达	
衣服	物品
a black T-shirt 一件黑色的T恤衫	a bunch of flowers 一束花
a white blouse 一件白色女衬衫	a pair of sunglasses 一副太阳镜
a beautiful dress 一件漂亮的裙子	pencils and erasers 铅笔和橡皮

续表

"购买的东西"相关表达	
衣服	物品
a pair of new jeans 一条新牛仔裤	rulers and crayons 尺子和蜡笔
a pair of trousers 一条裤子	brushes, and coloured pencils 画笔和彩色铅笔
a pair of shoes 一双鞋	some notebooks 一些笔记本
some pairs of socks 几双袜子	a book 一本书
a new hat 一顶新帽子	toys 玩具

邮件写作		
开头称呼	结束语	
Hi	See you soon	Take care
Hello	Write soon	Thanks
Hi + 英文名	Best regards	Cheers
Hello + 英文名	Best wishes	Yours
Dear + 英文名	Warm regards	
*英文名后要用英文逗号(,)，而不是中文分号(；)		

★必会句型★

1. 写信目的

I'm writing to you about ... 我写信给你是关于……

2. 购买什么东西

I'd like to buy ... 我想买……

3. 询问对方一起

Would you like to come with me? 你愿意和我一起去吗?

4. 见面时间和地点

1) We can meet ... 我们可以……见面。

2) How about meeting ...? ……见面怎么样?

Day 4　计划：博物馆之旅

 考场模拟

Your English friend Gina is coming with you to the local museum next Sunday.

Write an email to Gina.

Tell Gina:

- how you will travel to the museum

- what she can see at the museum

- what she needs to bring

Write 25 words or more.

思路点拨

Step 1:【审题，划重点】

弄清楚以下三点：

- 邮件写给谁

- 写邮件的原因

- 要回答的三个问题

Your English friend Gina is coming with you to the local museum next Sunday.

Write an email to Gina. ——— 要给她写邮件

写邮件的目的

Tell Gina:

- **how** you will **travel** to the museum

- **what** she can **see** at the museum

- **what** she needs to **bring**

要回答的3个问题

Step 2:【回答三个问题】

回答问题	how to travel 如何到	drive 开车　　　　give you a lift 捎你一程
		We will ... there, so we can ... 我们将……，所以我们可以……
	what to see 看到什么	art exhibits 艺术展览　　　historical artifacts 历史文物
		At the museum, you can see a variety of ... 在博物馆里，你可以看到各种各样的……

续表

| 回答问题 | what to bring
带什么 | comfortable shoes 舒适的鞋子 |
| | | Please make sure to bring ... as we will ...
请务必带……，因为我们要…… |

Step 3:【组句成段】

1. 表明写邮件目的：Looking forward to ...

2. 回答三个问题

3. 结尾语：See you soon.

Step 4:【检查修改】

☐ 1. 开头称呼和结束语正确   ☐ 2. 回答了3个问题

☐ 3. 词数≥25   ☐ 4. 无拼写错误

☐ 5. 无语法错误

📄 高分范文

Hi Gina,

I'm looking forward to our trip to the local museum next Sunday! We will drive there, so we can give you a lift. At the museum, you can see a variety of art exhibits and historical artifacts. It's a great opportunity to learn about our local history and culture. Please make sure to wear comfortable shoes and bring some water as we will do a lot of walking.

See you soon!

Jenny

（词数：74）

参考译文

嗨，吉娜：

我很期待下周日我们去当地博物馆的旅行！我们将开车去，所以我们可以捎你一程。在博物馆里，你可以看到各种各样的艺术展品和历史文物。这是了解我们当地历史和文化的好机会。请务必穿舒适的鞋子，带一些水，因为我们要走很多路。

到时见！

珍妮

考点锦囊

"搭便车"相关表达		
搭便车	give sb. a lift	I'll **give you a lift** to the station. 我用车顺便送你去车站。
	give sb. a ride	I missed the bus, can you **give me a ride** to the station? 我错过了公交车，你能顺便送我去车站吗？
（开车）接人	pick sb. up	I'll **pick** you **up** at five. 我五点钟来接你。

"博物馆"相关表达	
science museum 科学博物馆	national museum 国家博物馆
art museum 艺术博物馆	public museum 公立博物馆
history museum 历史博物馆	technology museum 科技博物馆
natural history museum 自然历史博物馆	military museum 军事博物馆
space museum 太空博物馆	insect museum 昆虫博物馆

出门游玩带的食物和装备	
食物	装备
a bottle of water 一瓶水	a helmet 一个头盔
some snacks and water 一些零食和水	a tennis racket 一个网球拍
some dessert and fruits 一些甜点和水果	a pair of sunglasses 一副太阳镜
a water bottle 一个水瓶	sunscreen 防晒霜

出门游玩带的衣服和物品	
物品	衣服
a mobile phone 一个手机	an extra coat 一件备用外套
a charger and power bank 充电器和充电宝	comfortable shoes 舒适的鞋
enough cash 足够的现金	a sleeping bag 一个睡袋
some money 一些钱	some shorts and a T-shirt 一些短裤和一件T恤
paintbrushes 画笔	some gym shoes 一些运动鞋

★*必会句型*★

1. **期待出行**

   1) I'm looking forward to ... 我很期待……

   2) Looking forward to our trip to ... next Sunday! 期待我们下周日的……之旅！

2. **出行方式**

   We will drive there. 我们将开车去。

3. **介绍博物馆的展品**

   At the museum, you can see ... 在博物馆里，你可以看到……

4. **学习的好机会**

   It's a great opportunity to learn about ... 这是了解……的好机会。

5. **需要携带的物品**

   Please make sure to bring ... 请务必带……

Day 5　请假：生病

 考场模拟

You have caught a cold. Write an email to your teacher, Miss Ellis.

In your email:

- ask your teacher for leave

- ask how to catch up on the progress

- ask if there is any homework

Write **25 words** or more.

 思路点拨

Step 1:【审题，划重点】

弄清楚以下三点：

- 邮件写给谁

- 写邮件的原因

• 要回答的三个问题

写邮件的目的

You **have caught a cold**. Write an email to your teacher, **Miss Ellis.** ——— 要给她写邮件

In your email,

- **ask** your teacher **for leave**
- **ask how to catch up on the progress**
- **ask** if there is any **homework**

要回答的3个问题

Step 2:【回答三个问题】

回答问题	ask for leave 请假	a day off 一天假
		May I ...? 我可以……吗?
	ask how to catch up on the progress 询问如何追赶进度	what we will study 我们学什么 fall behind 落后
		Could you let me know ...? 你能告诉我……?
	ask homework 询问作业	homework 家庭作业
		Please let me know if ... 如果……，请告诉我。

Step 3:【组句成段】

1. 表明写邮件目的：I'm sorry to tell you ...

2. 回答三个问题

3. 结尾语：Best regards,

Step 4:【检查修改】

☐ 1. 开头称呼和结束语正确　　☐ 2. 回答了3个问题

☐ 3. 词数≥25　　☐ 4. 无拼写错误

☐ 5. 无语法错误

高分范文

Dear Miss Ellis,

I'm sorry to tell you that I have caught a cold and I am feeling quite unwell. May I kindly request a day off tomorrow? Also, could you let me know what we will study tomorrow? I don't want to fall behind in class. Please let me know if I have any homework, too.

Best regards,

George

（词数：60）

参考译文

亲爱的埃利斯老师：

很抱歉告诉你，我感冒了，身体很不舒服。我明天可以请一天假吗？另外，你能告诉我明天要学什么吗？我不想在课堂上被落下。如果我也有家庭作业，请告诉我。

致敬

乔治

 考点锦囊

"健康状况" 相关表达		
生病	看医生	请假
get sick 生病	wear a mask 戴口罩	ask for leave 请假
feel unwell 感觉不舒服	see a doctor 看医生	three days off 三天休假
get / catch a cold 患感冒	dentist appointment 牙医预约	take two days off 请两天假
have a fever / temperature 发热	take some medicine 吃药	ask for two days' leave 请两天假
cough 咳嗽	get a shot 打针	
have a headache 头痛	in the hospital 在医院里	
have a sore throat 喉咙痛	in hospital 住院	
have a stomachache 肚子痛		
have a toothache 牙痛		

★必会句型★

1. 告知生病了

1) I'm sorry to tell you that I ... 很抱歉告诉你，我……

2) I'm feeling quite unwell. 我身体很不舒服。

2. 请假

1) May I kindly request a day off tomorrow? 我明天可以请一天假吗？

2) I need to take a day off from school tomorrow because I have a doctor's appointment. 我明天需要请一天假，因为我有个医生预约。

3) I regret to inform you that I am unable to attend school today due to illness. 很抱歉告知您，由于生病，我不能去上学。

4) I have caught a cold, and the doctor advised me to rest at home for a day. 我感冒了，医生建议我在家休息一天。

3. 问课程进度

1) Could you let me know what we will study tomorrow? 你能告诉我明天要学什么吗？

2) Could you please advise me how I can catch up on the progress? 你能告诉我怎样才能赶上进度吗？

3) I don't want to fall behind in class. 我不想在课堂上被落下。

4) I will make sure to catch up on any missed lessons. 我会确保赶上所有错过的课程。

4. 问作业

1) Please let me know if I have any homework, too. 如果我也有家庭作业，请告诉我。

2) Will there be any homework during my absence? 我不在的时候有作业吗？

Weekend 二 每周一练

I. 读一读，圈出正确的单词。

1. We have parties **at** / **in** New Year.

2. My birthday is **at** / **in** April.

3. I play basketball **in** / **on** Saturdays.

4. I often work **at** / **in** night.

5. I did my homework **in** / **at** two hours.

6. Let's meet **on** / **in** Saturday evening.

II. 选词填空。

meet	lend	need	grateful	go	forget

1. You _____ to bring your paintbrushes.

2. Can you _____ me a pencil, please?

3. Let's _____ at the bus stop.

4. I would be _____ if you could give me some help.

5. Do you want to _____ to the park?

6. I'm _____ that I can't go skating with you.

III. 将左右两列的相应内容连线，构成完整的一句话。

1. Would you   A. how I can get there.

2. Please tell me   B. like to come?

3. It will be great to   C. you're not busy.

4. I hope   D. go to the gym together.

5. My mum   E. lend me your skateboard tomorrow?

6. Could you please   F. will take me there.

IV. 改写句子，将括号中的词置于正确的位置。

1. It's a film. (funny)

   _____

2. I knew I had made a mistake. (big)

   _____

3. I don't know the city. (well)

   _____

4. We had lunch in a restaurant. (small)

   _____

5. He likes to eat chocolate. (a lot of)

   _____

6. Can you tell me a store? (cheap)

_____

7. A girl showed me the way to the bus stop. (kind)

_____

8. I haven't got money. (any)

_____

V. 写句子。对画线部分进行提问。

1. _____

I bought a book.

2. _____

I am going for a week.

3. _____

My favourite subject is history.

4. _____

They got there by subway.

5. _____

No, it didn't rain yesterday.

6. _____

She laughed because it was funny.

VI. 连词成句。

1. swimming, I, will, next, go, Saturday.

_____

2. cousin, My, swimming, loves.

_____

3. a, swimming pool, on, There's, Wood Road.

_____

4. I'm, a, going to, park, next, water, Saturday.

_____

5. get, can, the, bus , We.

_____

6. I, you, meet, at, the, bus, will, stop.

_____

7. is, near, the, The park, supermarket.

_____

8. friend, Paul, is, My, coming, too.

_____

邮件写作：
介绍过去经历&推荐

考试模块	时间	主题	内容	
		第3周目标		
	Day 1	经历：假期旅行	I had a fantastic holiday!	☐
	Day 2	经历：音乐会	The concert was fantastic!	☐
Part 6 邮件写作	Day 3	经历：自行车比赛	I recently participated in ...	☐
	Day 4	推荐：特别喜欢的食物	I want to share with you a special food ...	☐
	Day 5	推荐：最喜欢的电影	My favourite film must be ...	☐
	Weekend	每周一练	基础练习	☐

Day 1 　经历：假期旅行

 考场模拟

Read the email from your English friend, Maria.

From: Maria

I hope you had a pleasant holiday. Where did you go? What did you do? How was the weather there?

Write an email to Maria and answer the questions.

Write **25 words** or more.

 思路点拨

Step 1:【审题，划重点】

弄清楚以下三点：

- 邮件写给谁

- 写邮件的原因

● 要回答的三个问题

Read the email from your English friend, **Maria**. —— 要给她写邮件

From: Maria

I hope you had a pleasant **holiday**. **Where** did you go? **What** did you do? How was the

weather there?

要回答的3个问题

Write an email to Maria and **answer the questions.**

写邮件的目的

Step 2:【回答三个问题】

回答问题	where 去了哪里	Shanghai 上海		Beijing 北京
		I visited ... 我参观了……		
	what 做了什么	the Bund 外滩 the stunning skyline 令人惊叹的天际线 the Great Wall 长城 the Palace Museum 故宫博物院		
		In Shanghai, I explored ... and enjoyed ... 在上海，我游览了……并欣赏了…… In Beijing, I visited ... 在北京，我参观了……		
	weather 天气如何	sunny 晴朗的		warm 温暖的
		The weather was ... 天气是……		

Step 3:【组句成段】

    1. 表明邮件目的：I had a ...

    2. 回答三个问题

    3. 结尾语：Best wishes,

Step 4:【检查修改】

    □ 1. 开头称呼和结束语正确   □ 2. 回答了3个问题

    □ 3. 词数≥25   □ 4. 无拼写错误

    □ 5. 无语法错误

高分范文

Dear Maria,

I had a fantastic holiday! I visited Shanghai and Beijing. In Shanghai, I explored the Bund and enjoyed the stunning skyline. In Beijing, I visited the Great Wall and the Palace Museum. The weather was mostly sunny and warm. It was an unforgettable experience!

Best wishes,

Pat

（词数：49）

参考译文

亲爱的玛丽亚：

我度过了一个美妙的假期！我参观了上海和北京。在上海，我游览了外滩，欣赏了令人惊叹的天际线。在北京，我参观了长城和故宫。天气大多是晴朗而温暖的。这是一次难忘的经历！

祝好

帕特

 考点锦囊

"旅游城市和景点"相关表达	
Beijing 北京	**Shanghai 上海**
the Great Wall 长城	the Bund 外滩
the Palace Museum 故宫博物院	Yu Garden 豫园
the Summer Palace 颐和园	the Oriental Pearl Tower 东方明珠塔
Tiananmen Square 天安门广场	the Shanghai Disney Resort 上海迪士尼度假区

Xi'an 西安	**Hangzhou 杭州**
the Terracotta Army 兵马俑	the West Lake 西湖
the Ancient City Wall 古城墙	Lingyin Temple 灵隐寺
the Big Wild Goose Pagoda 大雁塔	the Six Harmonies Pagoda 六和塔
the Muslim Quarter 回民街	Longjing Tea Plantations 龙井茶园

Chengdu 成都	Guangzhou 广州
Chengdu Research Base of Giant Panda Breeding 成都大熊猫繁育研究基地	Canton Tower 广州塔
Wenshu Monastery 文殊院	the Chen Clan Ancestral Hall 陈家祠
Leshan Giant Buddha 乐山大佛	Sun Yat-sen Memorial Hall 中山纪念堂
Dujiangyan Irrigation System 都江堰	Chimelong Safari Park 长隆野生动物世界

描述天气的形容词			
春	夏	秋	冬
sunny 阳光充足的	hot 热的	windy 多风的	snowy 下雪的
clear 晴朗的	rainy 多雨的	foggy 多雾的	icy 冰冷的
warm 温暖的	wet 潮湿的	cloudy 多云的	dry 干燥的
mild 温和的		cool 凉爽的	

★必会句型★

1. 度过了美妙的假期

1) I had a fantastic holiday! 我度过了一个美妙的假期！

2) It was an unforgettable experience! 这是一次难忘的经历！

2. 介绍旅游城市和景点

1) I visited ... 我参观了……

2) I explored ... 我游览了……

3. 描述当时的天气

The weather was ... 天气是……

Day 2　经历：音乐会

 考场模拟

Read the email from your English friend, Alex.

From: Alex

Sorry I missed the concert yesterday. I hope you had a great time! Who did you go with?

What kind of music did the band play? What did you do after the concert?

Write an email to Alex and answer the questions.

Write **25 words** or more.

 ## 思路点拨

Step 1:【审题，划重点】

弄清楚以下三点：

- 邮件写给谁
- 写邮件的原因
- 要回答的三个问题

Read the email from your English friend, **Alex**. ——— 要给他写邮件

From: Alex

Sorry I missed the **concert** yesterday. I hope you had a great time! **Who** did you go with? **What kind of music** did the band play? **What** did you do after the concert?

写邮件的目的

要回答的3个问题

Write an email to Alex and **answer the questions**.

Step 2:【回答三个问题】

回答问题	who 谁	some friends 一些朋友
		I went to the concert with ... 我和……一起去了音乐会。
	what kind of music 什么类型的音乐	pop and rock music 流行和摇滚乐
		The band played ... 乐队演奏了……
	what 什么	went for dinner 吃晚饭
		After the concert, we ... 音乐会结束后，我们……

Step 3:【组句成段】

1. 表明邮件目的：The concert was ...

2. 回答三个问题

3. 结尾语：Take care,

Step 4:【检查修改】

☐ 1. 开头称呼和结束语正确　　☐ 2. 回答了3个问题

☐ 3. 词数≥25　　☐ 4. 无拼写错误

☐ 5. 无语法错误

📄 高分范文

Hi Alex,

The concert was fantastic! I went to the concert with some friends and we had a great time. The band played a mix of pop and rock music, and they were so cool. After the concert, we went for dinner and had a pleasant night. I wish you could have been there!

Take care,

Jack

（词数：57）

参考译文

嗨，亚历克斯：

音乐会太棒了！我和一些朋友去了音乐会，我们玩得很开心。乐队演奏了流行乐和摇滚乐的混合曲目，他们太酷了。音乐会结束后，我们去吃了晚饭，度过了一个愉快的夜晚。真希望你当时也在场！

保重

杰克

考点锦囊

"音乐类型" 相关表达	
classical music 古典音乐	light music 轻音乐
pop music 流行音乐	hip hop music 嘻哈音乐
rock music 摇滚音乐	country music 乡村音乐
jazz music 爵士音乐	R&B (rhythm and blues) 蓝调音乐

"休闲活动" 相关表达		
go to the zoo 去动物园	go hiking 去远足	visit a school 参观学校
go to the theatre 去剧院	go fishing 去钓鱼	visit the museum 参观博物馆
go to the concert 去听音乐会	go skating 去滑冰	watch TV 看电视
go to the cinema 去看电影	go skiing 去滑雪	watch a show 看表演
go shopping 去购物	have a snowball fight 打雪仗	surf the Internet 上网冲浪
go for a picnic 去野餐	make a snowman 堆雪人	plant trees 植树
have a picnic 野餐	join a club 加入一个社团	fly a kite 放风筝
have a barbecue 烧烤	listen to music 听音乐	climb a hill 爬山
pick fruits 采摘水果	draw a picture 画画	go for a bicycle ride 骑自行车兜风
go for a walk 散步	take a photo / picture 拍照	ride a horse 骑马
take a walk 散步	play hide and seek 玩捉迷藏	take a selfie 自拍

★必会句型★

1. 描述音乐会

The concert was fantastic! 音乐会太棒了!

2. 音乐会现场

1) The band played ... 乐队演奏了……

2) I went to the concert with ... 我和……去了音乐会。

3. 看音乐会的感受

1) We had a great time. 我们玩得很开心。

2) We had a fantastic time! 我们玩得很开心!

3) I wish you could have been there! 真希望你当时也在场!

4. 音乐会后的活动

After the concert, we ... 音乐会结束后，我们……

Day 3　经历：自行车比赛

 考场模拟

Read the email from your English friend, Mark.

> From: Mark
>
> How's it going. I heard you took part in a sports competition last weekend. Which sport was
>
> the competition for? How did you do in it? Why do you like this competition?

Write an email to Mark and answer the questions.

Write **25 words** or more.

思路点拨

Step 1:【审题，划重点】

弄清楚以下三点：

- 邮件写给谁
- 写邮件的原因
- 要回答的三个问题

Read the email from your English friend, **Mark**.　　——*要给他写便条*

> From: Mark
>
> How's it going. I heard you took part in **a sports competition** last weekend. **Which sport**
>
> was the competition for? **How** did you do in it? **Why** do you like this competition?

写邮件的目的　　　　　　　　*要回答的3个问题*

Write an email to Mark and **answer the questions**.

Step 2:【回答三个问题】

回答问题	which sport 哪类运动	a bicycle race 一场自行车比赛	
		I recently participated in ... 我最近参加了……	
	how 如何	pretty well 很好	in the top 10 前十名
		It was a thrilling experience! I did ... and managed to finish ... 这是一次激动人心的经历！我做得……，最终进入了……	

续表

回答问题	why 为什么	stay fit 保持健康　　　　　　enjoy the outdoors 享受户外活动
		I love this competition because it's a great way to ... 我喜欢这项比赛，因为它是……的好方法。

Step 3:【组句成段】

　　1. 表明邮件目的：I recently participated in a bicycle race. It was ...

　　2. 回答三个问题

　　3. 结尾语：Warm regards,

Step 4:【检查修改】

　　□ 1. 开头称呼和结束语正确　　　□ 2. 回答了3个问题

　　□ 3. 词数≥25　　　　　　　　　□ 4. 无拼写错误

　　□ 5. 无语法错误

高分范文

Hi Mark,

I recently participated in a bicycle race. It was a thrilling experience! I did pretty well and managed to finish in the top 10. I love this competition because it's a great way to stay fit and enjoy the outdoors.

Warm regards,

Nancy

（词数：45）

参考译文

　　嗨，马克：

　　我最近参加了一场自行车比赛。这是一次激动人心的经历！我做得很好，最终进入了前十名。我喜欢这项比赛，因为它是保持健康和享受户外活动的好方法。

诚挚的问候

南希

考点锦囊

"体育运动"相关表达		
球类运动	田径运动	其他运动
basketball 篮球	running 跑步	swimming 游泳
football 足球	jogging 慢跑	skating 滑冰
table tennis 乒乓球	high jump 跳高	skiing 滑雪
badminton 羽毛球	long jump 跳远	surfing 冲浪
baseball 棒球	jump rope 跳绳	cycling 自行车运动
volleyball 排球	marathon 马拉松	
tennis 网球		
*表示运动的名词前**不加the**，比如play basketball 打篮球		

喜欢运动的原因	
make new friends 交新朋友	idol 偶像
play with friends 与朋友一起玩耍	football idol 足球明星
keep fit 保持健康	active 活跃的
stay healthy 保持健康	enjoyable 有趣的
enjoy the view 欣赏风景	good exercise 有益的运动
very cool and interesting 很酷也很有意思	have outdoor adventures 进行户外冒险
gain confidence 获得自信	develop various skills 发展各种技能

★必会句型★

1. 最近的经历

1) I recently participated in a ... 我最近参加了一场……

2) The sports competition I took part in was ... 我参加的体育比赛是……

2. 描述经历

1) It was a thrilling experience! 这是一次激动人心的经历!

2) It was an unforgettable day for me. 对我来说，这是难忘的一天。

3. 比赛名次

1) I did well and managed to finish in the top ... 我做得很好，最终进入了前……名。

2) I won first place. 我赢得了第一名。

3) I won second place in my age group. 我赢得了年龄组第二名。

4. 喜欢的原因

1) I love this activity because it's a great way to ... 我喜欢这项活动，因为它是……的好方法。

2) I have always been a huge fan of ... 我一直是……的超级粉丝。

3) I enjoy this competition because it's competitive and allows me to showcase my basketball skills. 我喜欢这个比赛，因为它是竞争性的，让我展示我的篮球技术。

4) I love swimming because it's a challenging sport. 我喜欢游泳，因为这是一项富有挑战性的运动。

Day 4   推荐：特别喜欢的食物

 考场模拟

Write to your English friend Stephen describing a special food you like to eat.

Tell him:

- what the food is

- when you usually eat the food

- why you like this food

Write **25 words** or more.

 思路点拨

Step 1:【审题，划重点】

弄清楚以下三点：

- 邮件写给谁

- 写邮件的原因

- 要回答的三个问题

要给他写邮件　　　　写邮件的目的

Write to your English friend **Stephen** describing **a special food you like to eat**.

Tell him:

- **what** the food is
- **when** you usually eat the food ⎫ 要回答的3个问题
- **why** you like this food ⎭

Step 2:【回答三个问题】

回答问题	what 什么	hot pot 火锅 a popular Chinese dish 一道受欢迎的中国菜
		I wanted to share with you a special food that I really enjoy eating. It's called … 我想和你分享一种我非常喜欢吃的特别食物。它被称为……
	when 什么时候	chilly winter 寒冷的冬天
		I usually have hot pot during … 我通常在……吃火锅。
	why 为什么	tasty 美味的 bring friends and family together 把朋友和家人聚在一起
		I love it because it's … 我喜欢它，因为它……

Step 3:【组句成段】

1. 表明邮件目的：I wanted to share with you ...

2. 回答三个问题

3. 结尾语：Best regards,

Step 4:【检查修改】

☐ 1. 开头称呼和结束语正确　　　☐ 2. 回答了3个问题

☐ 3. 词数≥25　　　　　　　　　☐ 4. 无拼写错误

☐ 5. 无语法错误

📄 高分范文

Dear Stephen,

I want to share with you a special food that I really enjoy eating. It's called hot pot, a popular Chinese dish where you can cook your own ingredients in a flavourful broth. I usually have hot pot during the chilly winter. It's tasty, and brings friends and family together.

Best regards,

Alex

（词数：55）

参考译文

亲爱的斯蒂芬：

我想和你分享一种我非常喜欢吃的特别食物。它被称为火锅，一种很受欢迎的中国菜，你可以在香味浓郁的汤底中烹饪自己的食材。我通常在寒冷的冬天吃火锅。它很美味，还能让朋友和家人聚在一起。

诚挚的问候

亚历克斯

 考点锦囊

"中国美食" 相关表达	
Beijing roast duck 北京烤鸭	fried rice 炒饭
hot pot 火锅	rice 米饭
Cantonese roast goose 广东烧鹅	Mapo Tofu 麻婆豆腐
dumpling 饺子	shrimp dumpling 虾饺
moon cake 月饼	zongzi (rice-pudding) 粽子

"食物和饮料" 相关表达		
burger 汉堡包	cake 蛋糕	ice cream 冰激凌
sandwich 三明治	popcorn 爆米花	yogurt 酸奶
pasta 意大利面	candy 糖果	milk 牛奶
bread 面包	chocolate 巧克力	orange juice 橙汁
pizza 比萨饼	pie 派	soya milk 豆浆
French fries 炸薯条	salad 沙拉	coffee 咖啡

描述 "食物味道" 的形容词			
sour 酸的	spicy 辣的	delicious 美味的	silky 丝滑的
sweet 甜的	salty 咸的	tasty 口感好的	crispy 酥脆的
bitter 苦的	flavourful 美味的	juicy 多汁的	rich 油腻的

★ **必会句型** ★

1. 分享美食

I wanted to share with you a special food that I really enjoy eating. 我想和你分享一种我非常喜欢吃的特别食物。

2. 介绍美食的名字

It's called ..., a popular Chinese dish. 它被称为……，一种很受欢迎的中国菜。

3. 品尝美食的场景

I usually have ... during ... 我通常在……吃……

4. 推荐原因

It's tasty, and brings friends and family together. 它很美味，还能让朋友和家人聚在一起。

Day 5 · 推荐：最喜欢的电影

 考场模拟

Write an email to your English friend Maria. In your email, tell her about your favourite film.

- what kind of film it is
- what the film is about
- why introduce this movie

Write **25 words** or more.

 思路点拨

Step 1:【审题，划重点】

弄清楚以下三点：

- 邮件写给谁
- 写邮件的原因
- 要回答的三个问题

要给她写邮件　　写邮件的目的

Write an email to your English friend **Maria**. In your email, tell her about **your favourite film**.

- **what kind of film** it is
- **what the film is about**　　要回答的3个问题
- **why introduce this movie**

Step 2:【回答三个问题】

回答问题	what kind of film 什么类型的电影	*Harry Potter*《哈利·波特》 fantasy film 奇幻电影
		My favourite film must be … 我最喜欢的电影一定是……
	what the film is about 这部电影是关于什么的	a young wizard named Harry 一个名叫哈利的年轻巫师 adventures at Hogwarts school 霍格沃茨学校的奇遇
		It's a fantasy film about … 这是一部奇幻电影，讲述了……
	why introduce this movie 为什么介绍这部电影	magic 魔法 excitement 刺激
		I think you'd love it because it's filled with … 我想你会喜欢它的，因为它充满了……

Step 3:【组句成段】

1. 表明邮件目的：Well, my favourite film must be …

2. 回答三个问题

3. 结尾语：Yours,

Step 4:【检查修改】

- ☐ 1. 开头称呼和结束语正确　　☐ 2. 回答了3个问题
- ☐ 3. 词数≥25　　☐ 4. 无拼写错误
- ☐ 5. 无语法错误

📄 高分范文

Hi Maria,

Well, my favourite film must be *Harry Potter*. It's a fantasy film about a young wizard named Harry and his friends' adventures at Hogwarts school. I think you'd love it because it's filled with magic and excitement.

Yours,

Jimmy

（词数：41）

参考译文

你好，玛丽亚：

嗯，我最喜欢的电影是《哈利·波特》。这是一部奇幻电影，讲述了一个名叫哈利的年轻巫师和他的朋友们在霍格沃茨学校的冒险故事。我想你会喜欢它的，因为它充满了魔法和刺激。

你的吉米

🔔 考点锦囊

"电影类型" 相关表达	
action film 动作片	fantasy film 奇幻电影
comedy film 喜剧片	animated film 动画片
horror film 恐怖片	scary movie 恐怖电影
science fiction film 科幻片	drama film 剧情片
documentary 纪录片	romantic film 爱情片

"影片内容" 相关表达	
影片名	电影简介
Toy Story《玩具总动员》	*Toy Story* is **an animated film** about **the adventures and friendships of toys**.《玩具总动员》是一部关于玩具们的冒险和友谊的动画电影。
Coco《寻梦环游记》	*Coco* is **a heartwarming film** about **a young boy's adventurous journey to pursue his music dreams**.《寻梦环游记》是一部温暖人心的电影，讲述了一个小男孩追求音乐梦想的冒险之旅。
The Lion King《狮子王》	*The Lion King* is **a popular movie** about **a brave young lion who becomes king**.《狮子王》是一部很受欢迎的电影，讲述了一只勇敢的小狮子成为国王的故事。
*英文电影名，用英文斜体表示，不用中文书名号	

"评价影片" 相关表达	
funny 搞笑的	engaging 吸引人的
enjoyable 令人愉快的	inspiring 鼓舞人心的
exciting 令人兴奋的	Heartwarming 暖心的

续表

"评价影片" 相关表达	
adventurous 惊险的	fascinating 令人着迷的
amazing 令人惊叹的	make me laugh the whole time 让我笑个不停
amazing special effects 令人惊叹的特效	thrilling storyline 惊心动魄的故事情节

★ 必会句型 ★

1. 介绍喜欢的电影

1) My favourite film must be ... 我最喜欢的电影是……

2) I wanted to tell you about my all-time favourite film ... 我想告诉你我一直以来最喜欢的电影：《……》。

3) It's a comedy called ... 这是一部叫《……》的喜剧。

2. 概括电影内容

1) It's about a theme park with real-life dinosaurs. 它是关于一个有真实恐龙的主题公园。

2) It's about a boy who ... 它讲的是一个男孩……的故事。

3) It's a fantasy film about ... 这是一部奇幻电影，讲述了……

3. 推荐原因

1) I think you'd love it because it's filled with ... 我想你会喜欢它的，因为它充满了……

2) I love this movie because it's ... 我喜欢这部电影，因为它……

Weekend 二 每周一练

I. 读一读，圈出正确的单词。

1. I do my homework **at** / **in** the evening

2. Our holiday starts **on** / **in** 22 January.

3. She always goes shopping **at** / **on** the weekend.

4. I have lunch **at** / **in** noon.

5. We go on holiday **at** / **in** summer.

6. I usually wake up **at** / **in** 7 o'clock.

II. 用because、but、so填空。

1. We don't need to wear our coats _____ it's going to be hot today.

2. I am supposed to go cycling tomorrow, _____ I found my bike was broken.

3. We will finish at 4 p.m. _____ I can give it back to you after school.

4. I'm writing to you _____ I'm having a party tomorrow.

5. Jane has got a test tomorrow, _____ she has to study this evening.

6. By the end of the day we were tired _____ happy.

III. 将左右两列的相应内容连线，构成完整的一句话。

1. I'm going to the post office   A. great hot chocolate.

2. I need to go to the bank   B. with my dentist.

3. I should make an appointment   C. to borrow a book about art.

4. I'm going to the library   D. to get some medicine.

5. I must go to the chemist's   E. to get some cash.

6. That new cafe makes   F. to buy a stamp.

IV. 改写句子，将括号中的词置于正确的位置。

1. We wear jeans to school. (can't)

_____

2. I stay out late tonight. (would love to)

_____

3. We meet at six o'clock beside the town clock. (can)

_____

4. Sorry I go to the concert yesterday. (couldn't)

_____

5. You take some food. (should)

_____

6. Do you go to school on weekends? (have to)

_____

7. I arrive at the train station on Monday afternoon. (will)

   _____

8. I stay with an English friend next week. (am going to)

   _____

V. 写句子。对画线部分进行提问。

   1. _____

   No, he wasn't late.

   2. _____

   I'm reading.

   3. _____

   Yes, I'm going to Dave's party.

   4. _____

   We're going to stay in a tent!

   5. _____

   I go swimming once a week.

   6. _____

   I like classic music.

VI. 连词成句。

   1. about, meeting, What, at the station?

   _____

   2. very, you, I'm, will, me, go, with, pleased.

   _____

   3. can't, afraid, that, I, I'm, come.

   _____

   4. free, you, great, that, It's, are, on Sunday.

   _____

   5. on, Friday, go, instead, Can, we?

   _____

6. the, Let's, subway, meet, at, station.

_____

7. take, Why, together, don't, the, we, bus?

_____

8. forget, Don't, comfortable, to, wear, clothes.

_____

Week 4

邮件写作：
邀请&道歉&感谢&求助

考试模块	时间	主题	内容	
	Day 1	邀请：相约去动物园	Would you like to ...?	☐
	Day 2	道歉：无法去露营	I'm sorry I can't ...	☐
Part 6	Day 3	感谢：生日礼物	Thank you so much for ...	☐
邮件写作	Day 4	求助：借篮球	I am writing to ask if I could ...	☐
	Day 5	求助：笔记本	Could you please ...?	☐
	Weekend	每周一练	基础练习	☐

（表格标题：第4周目标）

Day 1   邀请：相约去动物园

 ### 考场模拟

You are planning to go to the zoo next Saturday.

Write an email to Paul and

- invite Paul to come

- say when you'd like to go

- tell Paul how to get there

Write **25 words** or more.

 ### 思路点拨

Step 1:【审题，划重点】

弄清楚以下三点。

- 邮件写给谁

- 写邮件的原因

• 要回答的三个问题

You are planning to **go to the zoo next Saturday**. ——— 写邮件的目的

Write an email to **Paul** and

要给他写邮件

• **invite** Paul to come

• say **when** you'd like **to go**

• tell Paul **how to get there**

要回答的3个问题

Step 2:【回答三个问题】

回答问题	invite 邀请	go to the zoo 去动物园
		Would you like to ...? 你愿意……吗?
	when 什么时候	10 a.m. 10点
		What about ...? ……如何?
	how to get there 怎么到那儿	take the No. 4 subway 乘地铁4号线
		You can ... 你可以……

Step 3:【组句成段】

1. 表明邮件目的：I'm going to the zoo next Saturday. Would you like to ...?

2. 回答三个问题

3. 结尾语：Write soon.

Step 4:【检查修改】

☐ 1. 开头称呼和结束语正确   ☐ 2. 回答了3个问题

☐ 3. 词数≥25   ☐ 4. 无拼写错误

☐ 5. 无语法错误

📧 高分范文

Hi Paul,

I'm going to the zoo next Saturday. Would you like to come with me? I heard you love pandas. What about meeting at 10 a.m.? You can take the No. 4 subway to get there.

Write soon.

Peter

（词数：40）

参考译文

嗨，保罗：

我下周六要去动物园。你愿意和我一起去吗？我听说你喜欢熊猫。上午十点见面怎么样？你可以乘地铁4号线到那里。

尽快回信。

彼得

 ## 考点锦囊

"交通"相关表达		
by bus 乘公交车	take a bus 乘公交车	take the Subway Line 1 乘地铁1号线
by taxi 乘出租车	take a taxi 乘出租车	take the No. 114 bus 乘114路交车
by car 乘汽车	take a cab 乘出租车	ride a bike 骑自行车
by train 乘火车	take the train 乘火车	on foot 步行
by subway 坐地铁	take a subway 乘地铁	walk 步行
by ship 乘船	take a ship 乘船	
by bike 骑自行车		
by plane / air 乘飞机		
* You can **take a bus** to get there. = You can get there **by bus**. 你可以坐公交车到那儿。		

"动物园的动物"相关表达			
lion 狮子	panda 熊猫	snake 蛇	peacock 孔雀
tiger 老虎	penguin 企鹅	zebra 斑马	dolphin 海豚
giraffe 长颈鹿	kangaroo 袋鼠	bear 熊	seal 海豹
elephant 大象	crocodile 鳄鱼	monkey 猴子	gorilla 大猩猩

★必会句型★

1. 出行计划

I'm going to ... next Saturday. 我下周六要去……

2. 邀请

Would you like to come with me? 你愿意和我一起去吗？

3. 见面时间和地点

1) What about meeting at ... o'clock? ⋯⋯点见面怎么样?

2) How about meeting at the park? 公园见面怎么样?

 Day 2 道歉: 无法去露营

 考场模拟

Your friend Lucy has asked you to go camping this Sunday. You can't go.

Write an email to Lucy.

Say:

- why you can't go

- when and where you can meet your friend next time

Write **25 words** or more.

思路点拨

Step 1:【审题,划重点】

弄清楚以下三点:

- 邮件写给谁

- 写邮件的原因

- 要回答的三个问题

写邮件的目的

Your friend Lucy has asked you to **go camping this Sunday.** You **can't go**.

Write an email to **Lucy**. ——— 要给她写邮件

Say:

- **why** you can't go

- **when** and **where** you can meet your friend next time.

要回答的3个问题

Step 2:【回答三个问题】

回答问题	why 为什么	visit my grandparents with my family 和家人去看我祖父母
		I'll ... 我将……
	when 什么时候	next Sunday 下周日
		Why don't we ...? 为什么我们不……?
	where 在哪里	sports centre 体育中心
		We can ... 我们可以……

Step 3:【组句成段】

1. 表明写信目的：I'm sorry ...

2. 回答三个问题

3. 结尾语：Best wishes,

Step 4:【检查修改】

☐ 1. 开头称呼和结束语正确　　☐ 2. 回答了3个问题

☐ 3. 词数≥25　　☐ 4. 无拼写错误

☐ 5. 无语法错误

📄 高分范文

Hi Lucy,

I'm sorry I can't go to the camping with you this Sunday. I'll visit my grandparents with my family that day. Why don't we meet next Sunday? We can play badminton in the sports centre.

Best wishes,

Mary

（词数：40）

参考译文

嗨，露西：

很抱歉这个星期天我不能和你一起去露营了。那天我要和家人去看望爷爷奶奶。我们下星期日见个面怎么样？我们可以在体育中心打羽毛球。

祝好

玛丽

考点锦囊

"无法赴约的原因" 相关表达		
visit my grandpa 看望我的爷爷	homework 家庭作业	bad weather 天气不好
birthday party 生日聚会	have an exam 有一场考试	safety concern 安全顾虑
family event 家庭活动	school work 学校作业	school activity 学校活动
feeling sick 生病了		

一周七天			
Monday 星期一	Wednesday 星期三	Friday 星期五	Sunday 星期日
Tuesday 星期二	Thursday 星期四	Saturday 星期六	weekend 周末
*在具体的某一天前用介词on，比如on Sunday（在周日）			

★必会句型★

1. 告知无法赴约

I'm sorry I can't ... with you. 很抱歉我不能和你一起……了。

2. 无法赴约的原因

I'll ... with my family that day. 那天我要和家人……

3. 改约时间

Why don't we meet next ...? 我们下个……见面怎么样？

4. 改约体育运动

We can ... in the sports centre. 我们可以在体育中心……

Day 3 　感谢：生日礼物

 考场模拟

Your friend, Sally, sent you a gift for your birthday. Write a note to Sally.

In your note:

- say thank you for the gift

- say why you like the gift

- tell her what you did for your birthday

Write **25 words** or more.

 ## 思路点拨

Step 1:【审题，划重点】

弄清楚以下三点：

- 便条写给谁

- 写便条的原因

- 要回答的三个问题

写便条的目的　　　　　　　　　　　　　　　　要给她写便条

Your friend, **Sally, sent you a gift** for your birthday. Write a note to **Sally**.

In your note:

- say **thank** you for the gift

- say **why** you like the gift　　　　　　要回答的3个问题

- tell her **what** you did for your birthday

Step 2:【回答三个问题】

回答问题	thank 感谢	lovely card 可爱的卡片 book 书
		Thank you so much for ... you sent me for my birthday. 非常感谢你在我生日时送给我的……
	why 为什么	thoughtful gift 体贴的礼物
		I absolutely love the book—it's ... 我非常喜欢这本书——它……
	what 什么	a wonderful day 美好的一天 a delicious dinner 美味的晚餐
		For my birthday, I spent ... with my family and enjoyed... 在我生日这天，我和我的家人度过了……，并享用了……

Step 3:【组句成段】

1. 表明便条目的：Thank you so much for ...

2. 回答三个问题

3. 结尾语：Best regards,

Step 4:【检查修改】

☐ 1. 开头称呼和结束语正确　　☐ 2. 回答了3个问题

☐ 3. 词数≥25　　☐ 4. 无拼写错误

☐ 5. 无语法错误

📄 高分范文

Dear Sally,

Thank you so much for the lovely card and book you sent me for my birthday. I really appreciate your thoughtful gift. I absolutely love the book—the author is one of my favourites! For my birthday, I spent a wonderful day with my family and enjoyed a delicious dinner.

Best regards,

Helen

（词数：55）

参考译文

亲爱的莎莉：

非常感谢你在我生日时送给我的可爱的卡片和书。我真的很感激你体贴的礼物。我非常喜欢这本书——它的作者是我最喜欢的作者之一！在我生日这天，我和我的家人度过了美好的一天，并享用了美味的晚餐。

祝好

海伦

 ## 考点锦囊

"礼物"相关表达	
a toy car 一辆玩具车	a beautiful drawing book 一本漂亮的画画书
a cute stuffed toy 一个可爱的毛绒玩具	a box of colourful crayons 一盒五颜六色的蜡笔
a toy robot 一个玩具机器人	a new colouring book 一本新的涂色书
a box of chocolates 一盒巧克力	a box of colourful markers 一盒五颜六色的马克笔
a bunch of flowers 一束花	a book 一本书
a beautiful necklace 一条漂亮的项链	

描述生日派对上的活动（过去式）	
sang birthday songs 唱生日歌 （sing的过去式是sang）	watched a movie 看电影 （watch的过去式是watched）
sang songs 唱歌 （sing的过去式是sang）	had a treasure hunt 玩寻宝游戏 （have的过去式是had）
blew out candles 吹蜡烛 （blow的过去式是blew）	played card games 玩纸牌游戏 （play的过去式是played）
ate the birthday cake 吃生日蛋糕 （eat的过去式是ate）	ate snacks 吃小吃 （eat的过去式是ate）
shared a birthday cake 分享生日蛋糕 （share的过去式是shared）	took photos 拍照片 （take的过去式是took）
danced 跳舞 （dance的过去式是danced）	enjoyed snacks and drinks 品尝小吃和饮料 （enjoy的过去式是enjoyed）

* 描述已经发生的事情，用动词的过去式，比如：

We **played** games, **sang** songs, and **had** a big birthday cake.

我们玩游戏，唱歌，吃了一个大的生日蛋糕。

* 描述未来将要发生的事情，用"will+动词原形"或"be going to +动词原形"，比如：

I **am going to have** a huge birthday cake and we **will play** games together!

我会吃一个大大的生日蛋糕，我们还要一起玩游戏！

★必会句型★

1. 表达感谢

1) Thank you so much for ... 非常感谢……

2) I really appreciate your thoughtful gift. 我真的很感激你体贴的礼物。

2. 表示礼物正合心意

1) I really liked this gift because I ... 我真的很喜欢这个礼物，因为我……

2) I absolutely love ... 我非常喜欢……

3) The colours are beautiful and it's exactly what I needed. 颜色很漂亮，这正是我所需要的。

3. 生日当天经历

1) For my birthday, I spent a wonderful day with my family. 在我生日这天，我和我的家人度过了美好的一天。

2) For my birthday, I enjoyed a delicious dinner. 在我生日这天，我享用了美味的晚餐。

Day 4 求助：借篮球

 考场模拟

You want to borrow your friend's basketball. Write an email to Alfie.

In your email:

* ask to borrow his basketball

* say why you need it

* tell him when you will return it

Write **25 words** or more.

 思路点拨

Step 1:【审题，划重点】

弄清楚以下三点：

* 邮件写给谁

* 写邮件的原因

* 要回答的三个问题

写邮件的目的   *要给他写邮件*

You want to **borrow your friend's basketball**. Write an email to **Alfie**.

In your email:

* **ask** to borrow his basketball

* say **why** you need it   *要回答的3个问题*

* tell him **when** you will return it

Step 2:【回答三个问题】

回答问题	ask 请求	borrow basketball 借篮球
		I am writing to ask if I could ... 我写信是想问我是否可以……
	why 为什么	got damaged 坏了 a friendly match 一场友谊赛
		My basketball ... , and I have ... on Saturday. 我的篮球……，星期六我有……

回答问题	when 什么时候	by Monday 星期一之前
		I promise to take good care of it and return it to you ... 我保证会好好保管它，并在……把它还给你。

Step 3:【组句成段】

    1. 表明写信目的：I am writing to ...

    2. 回答三个问题

    3. 结尾语：Looking forward to your reply.

Step 4:【检查修改】

    □ 1. 开头称呼和结束语正确   □ 2. 回答了3个问题

    □ 3. 词数≥25   □ 4. 无拼写错误

    □ 5. 无语法错误

高分范文

Dear Alfie,

I am writing to ask if I could borrow your basketball for a few days. My basketball got damaged, and I have a friendly match on Saturday. I promise to take good care of it and return it to you by Monday.

Looking forward to your reply.

Andrew

（词数：50）

参考译文

亲爱的阿尔菲：

我写信是想问我是否可以借用你的篮球几天。我的篮球坏了，星期六我有一场友谊赛。我保证会好好保管它，并在星期一之前把它还给你。

期待你的回信。

安德鲁

考点锦囊

"借东西&原因" 相关表达		
物品	借	原因
pencil 铅笔	I need to borrow **a pencil**. 我需要借一支铅笔。	I **forgot to bring mine**. 我忘记带我的了。
eraser 橡皮	Can I borrow **an eraser**, please? 我能借个橡皮吗?	I **can't find my eraser**. 我的橡皮找不着了。
ruler 尺子	May I borrow **a ruler**? 我可以借一把尺子吗?	I need it to **draw a straight line**. 我需要用它画一条直线。
book 书	Could I borrow **a book** from you? 我可以向你借一本书吗?	I want to **read something interesting**. 我想读一些有趣的东西。
paper 纸	Can I borrow **some paper**? 我可以借一些纸吗?	I **ran out of paper** for my drawing. 我的纸因为画画用完了。
notebook 笔记本	Is it possible to borrow **your notebook**? 我可以借一下你的笔记本吗?	I **was sick** yesterday and I didn't come to school. 我昨天生病了,没来上学。
glue 胶水	Could I borrow **some glue**? 我可以借一些胶水吗?	My artwork needs to **be stuck together**. 我的艺术作品需要粘在一起。
pen 钢笔	I need **a pen** because **mine doesn't work**. 我需要一支钢笔,因为我的坏了。	
paint 颜料	I'd like to borrow **some paint** to **finish my art project**. 我想借一些颜料来完成我的艺术项目。	

"将来的时间" 相关表达		
tomorrow 明天	next week 下周	in the future 在将来
the day after tomorrow 后天	next Monday 下周一	in a second 马上
morning 上午	next Tuesday 下周二	next time 下一次
noon 中午	next Wednesday 下周三	a few days later 几天后
afternoon 下午	next Thursday 下周四	in an hour's time 一小时内
evening 傍晚	next Friday 下周五	next Sunday 下周日
night 晚上	next Saturday 下周六	next weekend 下周末
tonight 今晚		
*Next可以用来表示时间上的顺序,意为"下一个的",比如next Thursday 下周四		

★必会句型★

1. 写信借东西

1) I am writing to ask if I could borrow your ... for a few days.

我写信是想问我是否可以借用你的……几天。

2) Can I borrow ..., please? 我能借……吗?

2. 借东西的原因

1) My ... got damaged. 我的……坏了。

2) I have ... on Saturday. 星期六我有……

3. 保证归还

1) I promise to take good care of it. 我保证会好好保管它。

2) I promise to return it to you by ... 我保证会在……之前把它还给你。

4. 期待回信

1) Looking forward to your reply. 期待你的回信。

2) I'm looking forward to your reply. 我期待着你的回信。

Day 5　求助：笔记本

考场模拟

Your friend, Ben, has got your notebook. Now you need it.

Write a note to Ben:

- ask for the notebook

- say why and when you need it

Write **25 words** or more.

思路点拨

Step 1:【审题，划重点】

弄清楚以下三点:

- 便条写给谁

- 写便条的原因
- 要回答的三个问题

写便条的目的

Your friend, Ben, **has got your notebook**. Now you **need it**.

Write a note to **Ben**: ———— 要给他写便条

- **ask for the notebook**
- say **why** and **when** you need it

要回答的3个问题

Step 2:【回答三个问题】

	ask for the notebook 要笔记本	the notebook 笔记本
回答问题		I need it now because ... 我现在需要它，因为……
	why 原因	an important test 一个重要的考试
		I need it for ... 我要用它……
	when 什么时候	the day after tomorrow 后天
		Could you please ... 你能……

Step 3:【组句成段】

1. 表明便条目的：I hope you're doing well! I just wanted to check if you still have ...

2. 回答三个问题

3. 结尾语：Thanks,

Step 4:【检查修改】

□ 1. 开头称呼和结束语正确　　　□ 2. 回答了3个问题

□ 3. 词数≥25　　　　　　　　　□ 4. 无拼写错误

□ 5. 无语法错误

📄 高分范文

Hi Ben,

I hope you're doing well! I just wanted to check if you still have my notebook. I need it for an important test the day after tomorrow. Could you please return it to me as soon as possible?

Your help would be greatly appreciated!

Thanks,

John

（词数：48）

参考译文

嗨，本：

希望你一切安好！我只是想确认我的笔记本是不是还在你那儿。我后天有一个重要的考试需要用它。你能尽快把它还给我吗？如蒙帮助，感激不尽。

感谢

约翰

 考点锦囊

"请归还&原因" 相关表达		
物品	归还	原因
textbook 课本	Could you please give back **my textbook**? 你能把我的课本还给我吗?	I need it back as I have to study for **an upcoming test**. 我需要它，因为我得准备即将到来的考试。
		Because I **have an important test** tomorrow. 因为我明天有一场重要的考试。
pen 钢笔	Could you please return **my pen**? 你能把我的钢笔还给我吗?	I need it for **taking notes in class**. 我需要它在课堂上记笔记。
book 书	Can you give back **my book**? 你能把我的书还给我吗?	**I haven't finished reading it yet**. 我还没有看完。
		I want to finish **reading it before the deadline**. 我想在截止日期前读完它。
pencil case 铅笔盒	Can you please return **my pencil case**? 你能把我的铅笔盒还给我吗?	I need it back because I **have important stationery inside**. 我需要拿回来，因为里面有很重要的文具。
headphones 耳机	Would you mind returning **my headphones**? 你介意把我的耳机还给我吗?	I **can't enjoy my music** without them. 没有它们我就无法享受音乐。
umbrella 雨伞	It would be great if you could give me back **my umbrella**. 如果你能把我的雨伞还给我就太好了。	The weather forecast says **it will rain today**. 天气预报说今天会下雨。

"归还时间"相关表达	
by Monday 在星期一以前	within one day 在一天之内
by Tuesday 在周二以前	within a day 在一天之内
by Wednesday 在周三以前	within two days 在两天之内
by Thursday 在周四以前	within three days 在三天之内
by Friday 在周五以前	within four days 在四天之内
by Saturday 在周六以前	within five days 在五天之内
by Sunday 在周日以前	within six days 在六天之内
by the end of the week 在本周末之前	as soon as possible 尽快

★必会句型★

1. 写信开头的问候语

I hope this letter finds you well. 希望你收到此信时一切安好。

2. 请求归还

1) I just wanted to check if you still have my ... 我只是想确认我的……是不是还在你那儿。

2) Could you please return my ...? 你能把我的……还给我吗？

3) Can you give back my ...? 你能把我的……还给我吗？

4) It would be great if you could give me back ... 如果你能把我的……还给我就太好了。

3. 归还原因

1) I need it for an important test the day after tomorrow. 我后天有一个重要的考试需要用它。

2) I need it back because ... 我需要拿回来，因为……

4. 告知归还时间

1) Could you please return it to me as soon as possible? 你能尽快把它还给我吗？

2) Please return it by ... 请在……之前归还。

3) Please make sure to return it no later than ... 请务必不迟于……归还。

5. 表示感激

Your help would be greatly appreciated! 如蒙帮助，感激不尽。

Weekend 三 每周一练

I. 读一读，圈出正确的单词。

1. We don't go to school **on** / **in** Sundays.

2. I go to school **on** / **in** the morning.

3. What do you do **at** / **in** the weekend?

4. My mother's birthday is **at** / **in** October.

5. I was born **in** / **at** 2013.

6. We meet **on** / **in** Tuesdays.

II. 选词填空。

| late | receive | violin | watched | afraid | promise |

1. He has just _____ a football match with his dad.

2. She usually plays the _____ in her spare time.

3. I was _____ for school because I missed the bus.

4. They are glad to _____ your message.

5. I _____ I will treat the skateboard well.

6. Don't _____ to wear comfortable shoes.

III. 将左右两列的相应内容连线，构成完整的一句话。

1. You need to bring some shorts

2. There is a boxing class

3. Can I walk, or will

4. Do the stores

5. Thanks for inviting me

6. I don't have much money,

A. which we could attend if you like.

B. so please tell me about a cheap store!

C. I need to take a bus or tram?

D. and a T-shirt plus some gym shoes.

E. to go camping during the school holiday.

F. stay open in the evenings?

IV. 改写句子，将括号中的词置于正确的位置。

1. She is happy! (always)

   _____

2. My sister plays the piano. (once a week)

   _____

3. I visit my grandmother at the weekend. (often)

   _____

4. My mother drives to work. (every day)

   _____

5. I have breakfast at 7 a.m. (usually)

   _____

6. I watch TV in the evening. (sometimes)

   _____

7. I go to the gym. (three times a week)

   _____

8. I will forget your kindness. (never)

   _____

V. 写句子。对画线部分进行提问。

1. _____

   I will arrive <u>at six o'clock.</u>

2. _____

   <u>Yes, they enjoyed the party.</u>

3. _____

   He went to <u>the cinema</u>.

4. _____

   We can meet <u>at six o'clock.</u>

5. _____

   I spoke to <u>my classmate</u>.

6. _____

I usually get <u>about an hour of</u> homework every day.

VI. 连词成句。

1. I'm, I, can't, come, to, afraid, your, party!

_____

2. sorry, I'm, I'll, be, a bit, but, late.

_____

3. this, I'm, going, to, a, see, movie, Saturday.

_____

4. come, Would, like, to, with, you, me?

_____

5. cinema, Shall, we, go, the, tomorrow, to, evening?

_____

6. you, come, to, want, too, Do?

_____

7. we, meet, at, the, How about, subway, station?

_____

8. meet, near, the, Let's, supermarket.

_____

Week 5

看图作文：日常生活

			第5周目标	
考试模块	时间	主题	内容	
Part 7 看图作文	Day 1	开学前一天	Lizzy was excited about her first day in school.	☐
	Day 2	整理卧室	Jenny's bedroom was in a mess.	☐
	Day 3	梦中吹气球	One night, a little girl lay in bed and went to sleep.	☐
	Day 4	猫打碎花瓶	One day, a cat was playing in the living room.	☐
	Day 5	邻里互助	Ted was doing his homework in his room.	☐
	Weekend	每周一练	基础练习	☐

Day 1　开学前一天

 考场模拟

Look at the three pictures.

Write the story shown in the pictures.

Write **35 words** or more.

 思路点拨

Step 1:【审题】

弄清楚以下三点：

- 图片中的主要人物是谁，并给人物命名
- 图片中的名词有哪些
- 图片中的动词有哪些

Step 2:【描述3幅图片】

图1	名词	Lizzy 丽兹 jeans 一条牛仔裤 backpack 双肩包	shirt 一件衬衫 chair 椅子 pencil box 铅笔盒
	动词	choose 选择（过去式chose） place 放置（过去式placed）	lay 放置，搁（过去式laid）
	组词成句	**Lizzy chose a shirt** to wear. **Lizzy chose a pair of jeans** to wear. **Lizzy laid** them **on a chair**. **Lizzy placed** her **pencil box** in her **backpack**.	
图2	名词	alarm 闹钟	6点 6 a.m.
	动词	set 设置（过去式set）	
	组词成句	She **set** her **alarm** for **6 a.m.**	
图3	名词	bed 床 smile 微笑	eye 眼睛 face 脸
	动词	climb 爬（过去式climbed）	fall asleep 入睡（过去式fell）
	组词成句	She **climbed** into **bed**. Her **eyes** shut and she **fell asleep**, with a **smile** on her **face**.	

Step 3:【组句成段】

1. 故事开头：Lizzy was excited about ...

2. 故事发展：分别叙述三张图片

3. 故事结尾：Finally, ...

Step 4:【检查修改】

□ 1. 三幅图的要点描述全面　　　　□ 2. 词数≥35

□ 3. 使用过去时讲述故事　　　□ 4. 动词的过去式正确

□ 5. 每个句子开头的首字母大写，名字首字母也大写

□ 6. 每个句子末尾都要加上句号(.)

📄 高分范文

Lizzy was excited about her first day in school. The night before, she chose a white shirt and a pair of blue jeans to wear and laid them on a chair. In her backpack, she placed her new pencil box with pencils. After brushing her teeth, she set her alarm for 6 a.m. and climbed into bed. Finally, her eyes shut and she fell asleep, with a smile on her face.

（词数：71）

参考译文

丽兹对她上学的第一天感到兴奋。前一天晚上，她选了一件白衬衫和一条蓝色牛仔裤，把它们放在椅子上。在她的背包里，她放了一个装有铅笔的新铅笔盒。刷完牙后，她把闹钟调到早上6点，爬上了床。最后，她闭上眼睛睡着了，脸上带着微笑。

考点锦囊

用"表示颜色的形容词"丰富句子		
初始句子	Lizzy chose a shirt and a pair of jeans to wear.	☆☆
修改后的句子	Lizzy chose a **white** shirt and a pair of **blue** jeans to wear.	☆☆☆☆

描述颜色的形容词		
white 白色的	black 黑色的	green 绿色的
red 红色的	golden 金色的	yellow 黄色的
orange 橙色的	purple 紫色的	grey 灰色的
pink 粉色的	blue 蓝色的	brown 棕色的

With的用法		
初始句子	Lizzy placed her pencil box in her backpack.	☆☆
修改后的句子	In her backpack, she placed her **new pencil box with pencils**.	☆☆☆☆

续表

With的用法

*with作介词

① **表示覆盖有或装有。**

Her shoes were covered **with** mud. 她的鞋上满是污泥。

The basket was stuffed **with** dirty clothes. 篮子里塞满了脏衣服。

② **意为"有；具有；带有"。**

a girl **with** red hair = a girl who has red hair 一位红发女孩

a coat **with** a hood 带兜帽的外套

a boy **with** a suitcase 提衣箱的男孩

a book **with** a blue cover 一本蓝色封面的书

"学校学习"相关表达		
名词词组	动词词组	介词词组
primary school 小学	keep quiet 保持安静	after school 放学后
middle school 中学	clean up 打扫干净	before school 上学前
school uniform 校服	prepare for 为……做准备	in class 在课堂上
classroom activity 课堂活动	study hard 努力学习	after class 下课后
pencil case 铅笔盒	keep a diary 写日记	during the break 在休息期间
library card 图书卡	take an exam 参加考试	at lunchtime 在午餐时间
school textbook 学校教科书	take the finals 参加毕业考试	on the desk 在桌子上
a piece of paper 一张纸	enter a school 入学	on the table 在桌子上
school project 学校项目	feel nervous 感到紧张	on the wall 在墙上
sports lesson 体育课	get nervous 变得紧张	in the classroom 在教室里
music class 音乐课	make mistakes 犯错误	in the backpack 在背包里

★必会句型★

1. 心情描述

Lizzy was excited about ... 丽兹感到兴奋……

2. 开心入睡

She fell asleep with a smile on her face. 她面带微笑睡着了。

Day 2　整理卧室

 考场模拟

Look at the three pictures.

Write the story shown in the pictures.

Write **35 words** or more.

思路点拨

Step 1:【审题】

　　弄清楚以下三点：

- 图片中的主要人物是谁，并给人物命名
- 图片中的名词有哪些
- 图片中的动词有哪些

Step 2:【描述3幅图片】

图1	名词	Jenny 珍妮 mess 杂乱，不整洁	in a mess 杂乱不堪
	动词	is 是（过去式was）	
	组词成句	Jenny's bedroom **was in a mess**.	
图2	名词	thing（不具体指称的）东西 sheet 床单	closet 壁橱 blanket 毯子

续表

图2	动词	put 放（过去式put）
	组词成句	Jenny put the **things** in the **closet**. Jenny pulled the **sheet** and **blanket**, making them smooth.
图3	名词	pillows 枕头　　　　　　　bed 床 doll 玩具娃娃　　　　　　mom 妈妈
	动词	place 放（过去式placed）　　make 做（过去式made） say 说（过去式said）　　　do 做（过去式did）
	组词成句	Jenny **placed** the **pillows** neatly on the head of the **bed**. Jenny **made** the **doll** sit quietly on the **bed**. **Mom said** she **did** a great job.

Step 3:【组句成段】

1. 故事开头：Jenny's bedroom was ...

2. 故事发展：分别叙述三张图片

3. 故事结尾：Mom said ...

Step 4:【检查修改】

□ 1. 三幅图的要点描述全面　　　□ 2. 词数≥35

□ 3. 使用过去时讲述故事　　　　□ 4. 动词的过去式正确

□ 5. 每个句子开头的首字母大写，名字首字母也大写

□ 6. 每个句子末尾都要加上句号(.)

📄 高分范文

　　Jenny's bedroom was in a mess. First, she put the things in the closet. Then, she pulled the sheet and blanket, making them smooth. Next, she placed the pillows neatly on the head of the bed. Finally, Jenny made the doll sit quietly on the bed. Mom said she did a great job.

（词数：53）

参考译文

　　珍妮的卧室一团糟。首先，她把东西放在壁橱里。然后，她拉了拉床单和毯子，把它们弄平。接着，她把枕头整齐地放在床头。最后，珍妮让娃娃安静地坐在床上。妈妈说她做得很好。

考点锦囊

表示"时间顺序"和"事情发展顺序"的连接词		
首先	其次	最后
first 首先	then 然后	finally 最后
firstly 首先	next 紧接着；随后	at last 最后
in the first place 首先	later 随后	in the end 最后
to start with 首先	second 其次	eventually 最终

"做家务"动词词组		
make a bed 整理床铺	wash the dishes 洗碗	wash clothes 洗衣服
clean the room 打扫房间	do the cooking 做饭	do the laundry 洗衣服
clean the windows 擦窗户	cook the meal 做饭	hang out the clothes 晒衣服
clean the floor 擦地板	make dinner 做晚餐	fold clothes 叠衣服
sweep the floor 清扫地板	water the flowers 浇花	wash the car 洗车
clean the yard 打扫院子	feed the pet 喂宠物	

"家居"介词词组		
in the bedroom 在卧室里	on the bed 在床上	near the sofa 在沙发旁边
in the kitchen 在厨房里	under the bed 在床下	near the window 在窗户旁边
in the living room 在客厅里	on the dresser 在梳妆台上	behind the door 在门后面
in the bathroom 在浴室里	on the floor 在地板上	
in the closet 在壁橱里	on the balcony 在阳台上	
in the yard 在院子里		
in the corner 在角落里		

★必会句型★

1. **卧室整洁**

   1) Her bedroom was in a mess. 她的卧室一团糟。

   2) Her bedroom was tidy. 她的卧室很整洁。

2. 被表扬

... said she did a great job. ……说她做得很好。

 Day 3   梦中吹气球

 考场模拟

Look at the three pictures.

Write the story shown in the pictures.

Write **35 words** or more.

思路点拨

Step 1:【审题】

弄清楚以下三点：

- 图片中的主要人物是谁，并给人物命名

- 图片中的名词有哪些

- 图片中的动词有哪些

Step 2:【描述3幅图片】

图1	名词	night 晚上 bed 床	little girl 小女孩 sleep 睡觉
	动词	lie 躺（过去式lay）	go 走（过去式went）
	组词成句	One **night**, a **little girl lay** in **bed** and went to **sleep**.	
图2	名词	dream 梦 balloon 气球	beach 海滩
	动词	sit 坐（过去式sat）	blow 吹（过去式blew）
	组词成句	In her dream, she **sat** on the **beach** and **blew** a **balloon**.	
图3	名词	huge balloon 大气球	
	动词	push 推（过去式pushed）	push over 推倒
	组词成句	The **huge balloon pushed** her **over**.	

Step 3:【组句成段】

1. 故事开头：One night, ...

2. 故事发展：分别叙述三张图片

3. 故事结尾：It was truly a terrible dream.

Step 4:【检查修改】

☐ 1. 三幅图的要点描述全面 ☐ 2. 词数≥35

☐ 3. 使用过去时讲述故事 ☐ 4. 动词的过去式正确

☐ 5. 每个句子开头的首字母大写，名字首字母也大写

☐ 6. 每个句子末尾都要加上句号(.)

📄 高分范文

One night, a little girl lay in bed and went to sleep. In her dream, she sat on the beach and blew a balloon. The balloon got bigger and bigger. But then, the huge balloon pushed her over and she couldn't breathe. It was truly a terrible dream.

（词数：48）

参考译文

一天晚上，一个小女孩躺在床上睡着了。在她的梦里，她坐在沙滩上吹了一个气球。气球变得越来越大。但随后，巨大的气球把她推倒了，她无法呼吸。这真是一个可怕的梦。

 考点锦囊

形容词比较级		
表示"越来越……"	形容词比较级 + and + 形容词比较级（单音节形容词）	bigger and bigger 越来越大
	more and more + 形容词原级（多音节形容词）	more and more beautiful 越来越美丽

描述心情的形容词			
正面情绪		负面情绪	
happy 高兴的	overjoyed 非常高兴的	sad 悲伤的	anxious 焦虑的
glad 高兴的	excited 兴奋的	unhappy 不高兴的	awful 糟糕的
joyful 充满喜悦的	content 满足的	bad 坏的	nervous 紧张的
pleased 高兴的	satisfied 满意的	afraid 害怕的	tired 疲劳的
cheery 心情愉快的	hopeful 充满希望的	terrible 可怕的	hopeless 绝望的
delighted 非常高兴的		nervous 紧张的	helpless 无助的
		worried 担心的	

push相关词组	
push on 继续前进（或进行活动）	They rested for a while then **pushed on** to the next camp. 他们休息了一会，然后继续朝下一个营地迈进。
push sb. over 把某人推倒	Tom **pushed** me **over** in the playground. 汤姆在运动场上把我推倒了。
push in 插队	A couple of boys **pushed in** at the head of the queue. 几个男孩插到了队伍的最前面。
push aside 不考虑；不去想	She **pushed aside** the feelings of fear. 她排除了恐惧。

★必会句型★

做梦

1) In her dream, she ... 在梦中，她……

2) It was truly a / an ... dream. 那真是一场……梦。

Day 4　猫打碎花瓶

 考场模拟

Look at the three pictures.

Write the story shown in the pictures.

Write **35 words** or more.

思路点拨

Step 1:【审题】

　　　弄清楚以下三点：

- 图片中的主要人物是谁，并给人物命名

- 图片中的名词有哪些

- 图片中的动词有哪些

Step 2:【描述3幅图片】

	名词	cat 猫	living room 客厅
图1	动词	is 是（过去式was）	play 玩（现在分词playing）
	组词成句	A **cat was playing** in the **living room**.	
	名词	vase 花瓶	table 桌子
图2	动词	break 打破（过去式broke） run away 逃跑	run 跑（过去式ran）
	组词成句	The cat **broke** the **vase** on the **table**. The cat was frightened and **ran away**.	
	名词	woman 女人 floor 地板	broken vase 打碎的花瓶
图3	动词	come 来（过去式came） come back 返回	see 看（过去式saw）
	组词成句	The **woman came back**. She **saw** the vase **broken** on the **floor**.	

Step 3:【组句成段】

1. 故事开头：One day, ...

2. 故事发展：分别叙述三张图片

3. 故事结尾：She was very angry ...

Step 4:【检查修改】

☐ 1. 三幅图的要点描述全面　　　　☐ 2. 词数≥35

☐ 3. 使用过去时讲述故事　　　　　☐ 4. 动词的过去式正确

☐ 5. 每个句子开头的首字母大写，名字首字母也大写

☐ 6. 每个句子末尾都要加上句号(.)

高分范文

One day, a cat was playing in the living room. Suddenly, it broke the vase on the table. The cat was frightened and ran away quickly. When the woman came back, she saw the vase broken on the floor. She was very angry and punished the cat.

（词数：47）

参考译文

一天，一只猫在客厅里玩耍。突然，它打翻了桌上的花瓶。猫吓了一跳，飞快地跑开了。当那个女人回来时，她看见花瓶摔在地上。她非常生气，惩罚了那只猫。

 考点锦囊

描述故事中的意外或惊喜		
副词	名词词组	介词词组
really 真正地	surprise package 意外包裹	to one's surprise 令某人惊讶的是
suddenly 突然地	surprising news 惊人的消息	to one's joy 令某人高兴的是
unexpectedly 出乎意料地	delightful surprise 令人高兴的惊喜	to one's delight 令某人高兴的是
surprisingly 令人惊讶地	amazing discovery 惊人的发现	by accident 意外地
quickly 迅速地	unexpected surprise 意外的惊喜	by chance 碰巧地
	unexpected event 意外事件	

A2 Key中既是名词又是动词的单词		
break	n. 间歇；休息	a **break** for lunch 午休时间
	v. 打破	Someone has **broken** the window. 有人打破了窗户。
book	n. 书	a good **book** 一本好书
	v. 预订	**book** a place 预订一个位置
call	n. 电话	I'm waiting for a **call** from Anna. 我在等安娜的电话。
	v. 打电话	I'll **call** the phone again later this afternoon. 今天下午晚些时候我再打电话。
delay	n. 延误	There will be a **delay** of two hours. 将晚点两小时。
	v. 延迟	The flight is **delayed**. 航班延误了。
fall	n. 秋天	in the **fall** 在秋天
	v. 跌倒	He **fell** and hurt his leg. 他摔了一跤，伤了腿。
order	n. 订单	We have received your **order**. 我们已经收到你的订单。
	v. 点（酒菜等）	She **ordered** her meal from the waiter. 她向服务员点了餐。
race	n. 比赛	a running **race** 跑步比赛
	v. 参加比赛	He **raced** to a thrilling victory in the relay. 他在接力赛中取得了激动人心的胜利。
return	n. 归来	my **return** from holiday 我度假归来
	v. 回来	He **returned** home late. 他回家晚了。

续表

A2 Key中既是名词又是动词的单词		
ring	*n.* 戒指	a gold **ring** 一枚金戒指
	v. 给……打电话	I'll **ring** you up later. 我之后再给你打电话。

come相关词组	
come back 返回	We **came back** from our holiday yesterday. 我们昨天度假回来了。
come in 到达	The train is **coming in** now. 火车现在进站。
come on 开始	It **came on** to rain. 天下起雨来了。
come out（太阳、月亮或星星）出现，露出	The rain stopped and the sun **came out**. 雨停后太阳出来了。
come across（偶然）遇见	He **came across** some old photographs in a drawer. 他在抽屉里偶然发现了一些旧照片。

★必会句型★

1. 玩耍

One day, ... was / were playing in the living room. 一天，……正在客厅里玩。

2. 心情描述

She was very ... 她非常……

Day 5 邻里互助

 考场模拟

Look at the three pictures.

Write the story shown in the pictures.

Write **35 words** or more.

思路点拨

Step 1:【审题】

弄清楚以下三点：

- 图片中的主要人物是谁，并给人物命名
- 图片中的名词有哪些
- 图片中的动词有哪些

Step 2:【描述3幅图片】

图1	名词	Ted 特德 neighbour 邻居	homework 家庭作业 fire 火	window 窗户 on fire 着火
	动词	is 是（过去式was） look 看（过去式looked）	do 做（现在分词doing） see 看见（过去式saw）	
	组词成句	**Ted was doing** his **homework** in his room. He **looked** out of the **window**. He **saw** his **neighbour**'s house **on fire**.		
图2	名词	father 爸爸		
	动词	tell 告诉（过去式told）	call 打电话（过去式called）	
	组词成句	The boy **told** his **father** that there was a fire. His **father called** the fire department.		
图3	名词	firefighter 消防员		
	动词	come 来（过去式came）	put 放（过去式put）	put out 扑灭（火焰）
	组词成句	The **firefighters came** and **put out** the fire.		

Step 3:【组句成段】

1. 故事开头：Ted was ...

2. 故事发展：分别叙述三张图片

3. 故事结尾：Ted felt proud ...

Step 4:【检查修改】

☐ 1. 三幅图的要点描述全面   ☐ 2. 词数≥35

☐ 3. 使用过去时讲述故事   ☐ 4. 动词的过去式正确

☐ 5. 每个句子开头的首字母大写，名字首字母也大写

☐ 6. 每个句子末尾都要加上句号(.)

📄 高分范文

Ted was doing his homework in his room. When he looked out of the window, he saw his neighbour's house on fire. The boy walked to the living room and told his father that there was a fire. His father called the fire department at once. The firefighters came quickly and eventually put out the fire. Ted felt proud that he had helped in some way.

（词数：66）

参考译文

特德正在他的房间里做作业。当他向窗外看时，他看到邻居的房子着火了。男孩走到客厅，告诉他的父亲发生了火灾。他的父亲立刻打电话给消防部门。消防员很快赶来，最终将火扑灭。特德为自己在某种程度上提供了帮助而感到自豪。

🔔 考点锦囊

表示立即、迅速做某事		
副词	介词短语	
immediately 立即，立刻	at once 立即，马上	in a moment 立刻
instantly 立即，即刻	right away 立即，马上	at the moment 此刻
promptly 迅速地，立即	without delay 毫不延迟，立即	for a moment 片刻，一会儿
quickly 迅速地，立即	without hesitation 毫不犹豫地	for a while 一会儿
speedily 迅速地，立即	in a hurry 匆忙地，立即	for the moment 暂时

look相关词组	
look after 照顾，照料	My sister will **look after** my cat while I'm on vacation. 我度假期间，我妹妹会照顾我的猫。
look at 看	**Look at** the time! We'll be late. 看几点了！我们要迟到了。

look相关词组	
look for 找	He was **looking for** his keys. 他在找他的钥匙。
look out 小心，当心	**Look out**! There's a car coming! 当心！有一辆汽车开过来了！
look forward to 盼望，期待	I'm **looking forward to** the weekend. 我盼着过周末呢。

★必会句型★

1. 写作业

... was doing his homework. ……正在写作业。

2. 心情描述

Ted felt proud that ... 特德为……感到自豪。

Weekend 二 每周一练

I. 写出下列动词的过去式。

1. is _____
2. do _____
3. go _____
4. call _____
5. come _____
6. look _____

7. make _____
8. put _____
9. run _____
10. say _____
11. see _____
12. tell _____

II. 读一读，圈出正确的单词。

1. I couldn't see well **because** / **but** it was cloudy.

2. I wanted to go shopping, **but** / **so** I didn't have any money.

3. He went to a store, **so** / **but** it was closed.

4. It was sunny, **but** / **so** they decided to have a barbecue.

5. He woke up **and** / **or** got out of bed.

6. She opened the fridge, **but** / **because** it was almost empty.

7. Jane was hungry, **but** / **so** she decided to go out for some food.

8. We couldn't play tennis **but / because** it was raining!

III. 选词填空。

| ran | shouted | relaxed | played | made | watched |

1. I _____ a film at home last night.

2. He _____ into the room and picked up the phone.

3. I _____ for help but nobody came.

4. They _____ a poster and wrote invitations.

5. Jake _____ the piano and they sang together.

6. Max sat down and _____ for a while.

IV. 将左右两列的相应内容连线，构成完整的一句话。

1. It was late   A. so Dan put on his coat.

2. It was cold   B. with her family.

3. Janet was on holiday   C. some new shoes.

4. He wanted to buy   D. that my hat came off!

5. It was so windy   E. my friends all night.

6. I chatted with   F. and I was very tired.

V. 判断下面句子正误，如有错，请圈出并将正确形式写在下面的横线上。

1. He and his family have a picnic yesterday.   ☐

   _____

2. They go to a music concert last night.   ☐

   _____

3. We haven't got any homeworks tonight.   ☐

   _____

4. The children were playing happily in the garden.   ☐

   _____

5. She eats a lot of chocolates. ☐

_____

6. He read the invitation carefully. ☐

_____

VI. 用连接词把下面两个句子合并为一句。

1. He had two tickets for the new film.

   It starts at 10:30.   (which)

   _____

2. They were talking about a film.

   They watched a film yesterday.   (that)

   _____

3. They saw a girl.

   She was holding a map.   (who)

   _____

4. She saw some black shoes.

   She liked the shoes.   (which)

   _____

5. Ketty saw a girl.

   She looked scared.   (who)

   _____

6. He spoke to a waiter.

   The waiter worked in the restaurant.   (who)

   _____

7. She took off the coat.

   She was wearing the coat.   (which)

   _____

8. The old woman was carrying a bag.

   It looked heavy.   (which)

   _____

看图作文：休闲活动

第6周目标				
考试模块	时间	主题	内容	
Part 7 看图作文	Day 1	跑步比赛	One day, a boy named Jack was going to take part in a school running race.	☐
	Day 2	放风筝	One sunny day, Nick's dad and Nick made a kite together.	☐
	Day 3	画画乐事	One day, a little boy was joyfully painting a beautiful picture.	☐
	Day 4	购物小帮手	On Saturday, Mark's mother sent him to go shopping.	☐
	Day 5	生日惊喜	On my last birthday, my family and friends surprised me with a magical birthday party.	☐
	Weekend	每周一练	基础练习	☐

Day 1　跑步比赛

 考场模拟

Look at the three pictures.

Write the story shown in the pictures.

Write **35 words** or more.

思路点拨

Step 1:【审题】

弄清楚以下三点：

- 图片中的主要人物是谁，并给人物命名
- 图片中的名词有哪些
- 图片中的动词有哪些

Step 2:【描述3幅图片】

图1	名词	Jack 杰克 running race 跑步比赛	boy 男孩 starting line 起跑线	
	动词	is 是（过去式was） is going to 将要		
	组词成句	One day, a **boy** named Jack **was going to** take part in a school **running race**. At the **starting line**, he **was** nervous but ready.		
图2	名词	halfway point 中间点 crowd 人群	in the lead 处于领先地位 cheer 欢呼声	
	动词	keep 保持（过去式kept）		
	组词成句	At the **halfway point**, he was still **in the lead**. The **cheers** from the **crowd kept** him going.		
图3	名词	gold medal 金牌		
	动词	win 赢（过去式won）		
	组词成句	In the end, he **won** the **gold medal**!		

Step 3:【组句成段】

1. 故事开头：One day, ...

2. 故事发展：分别叙述三张图片

3. 故事结尾：He was so ...

Step 4:【检查修改】

- □ 1. 三幅图的要点描述全面
- □ 2. 词数≥35
- □ 3. 使用过去时讲述故事
- □ 4. 动词的过去式正确
- □ 5. 每个句子开头的首字母大写，名字首字母也大写
- □ 6. 每个句子末尾都要加上句号(.)

高分范文

One day, a boy named Jack was going to take part in a school running race. At the starting line, he was nervous but ready. At the halfway point, he was still in the lead. The cheers from the crowd kept him going and he gave it his all. In the end, he crossed the finish line first and won the gold medal! He was so happy!

（词数：67）

参考译文

一天，一个叫杰克的男孩要参加学校的跑步比赛。在起跑线上，他很紧张，但准备好了。在半路上，他处于领先地位。人群的欢呼声让他继续前进，他全力以赴。最后，他第一个冲过终点，赢得了金牌！他太高兴了！

考点锦囊

"比赛"相关表达		
spectator 观众	starting line 起跑线	start the race 开始比赛
audience 观众	midway point 中途点	participate in a race 参加比赛
crowd 人群；观众	halfway point 中途点	train for a competition 为比赛而训练
cheer 欢呼	finishing line 终点线	go ahead in the match 在比赛中领先
clap 鼓掌	training session 训练课程	win the game 赢得比赛
ranking 名次	result of the match 比赛结果	lose the game 输掉比赛
place 名次	first place 第一名	lead in the match 比赛领先
champion 冠军	second place 第二名	false start 抢跑
winner 获胜者	third place 第三名	
medal 奖牌	warm-up 热身；（赛前）准备活动	

take相关词组	
take off 脱下（衣物）	She **took off** her shoes. 她脱下鞋子。
take off 起飞	The plane **took off** an hour late. 飞机起飞晚了一小时。
take part in 参加	She often **takes part in** any of the class activities. 她经常参加班里的所有活动。
take away 带回食用；买外卖食物	Two burgers to **take away**, please. 请来两份汉堡包，带走。

give相关词组	
give back 归还	I picked it up and **gave** it **back** to him. 我把它捡起来还给了他。
give up 放弃	She doesn't **give up** easily. 她决不轻易认输。
give out 分发	The teacher **gave out** the exam papers. 老师分发了试卷。
give (sth.) your all 全力以赴（做某事）	We must be finished by tonight, so I want you to **give it your all**. 我们今晚一定要做完，所以我希望你们会全力以赴。

★ 必会句型 ★

1. 过去将要做某事

One day, a boy named Jack was going to ... 一天，一个叫杰克的男孩要……

2. 心情描述

He was so happy! 他太高兴了!

Day 2　放风筝

考场模拟

Look at the three pictures.

Write the story shown in the pictures.

Write **35 words** or more.

思路点拨

Step 1:【审题】

弄清楚以下三点：

- 图片中的主要人物是谁，并给人物命名
- 图片中的名词有哪些
- 图片中的动词有哪些

  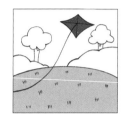

Step 2:【描述3幅图片】

图1	名词	Nick 尼克 kite 风筝 paper 纸	Nick's dad 尼克的爸爸 bamboo stick 竹棍 rope 绳子
	动词	make 做（过去式made）	use 用（过去式used）
	组词成句	**Nick's dad** and **Nick made a kite** together. They **used** a **bamboo stick**, some **paper**, and several **ropes**.	
图2	名词	park 公园	
	动词	take 拿（过去式took）	
	组词成句	They **took** it to the **park** to fly.	
图3	名词	sky 天空	
	动词	fly 飞（过去式flew）	
	组词成句	The kite **flew** high in the **sky**.	

Step 3:【组句成段】

1. 故事开头：One sunny day, ...

2. 故事发展：分别叙述三张图片

3. 故事结尾：Nick was so ...

Step 4:【检查修改】

□ 1. 三幅图的要点描述全面 □ 2. 词数≥35

□ 3. 使用过去时讲述故事 □ 4. 动词的过去式正确

□ 5. 每个句子开头的首字母大写，名字首字母也大写

□ 6. 每个句子末尾都要加上句号(.)

高分范文

One sunny day, Nick's dad and Nick made a kite together. They used a bamboo stick, some colourful paper, and a long string. After finishing the kite, they took it to the park to fly. The kite flew high in the sky like a bird. Nick was so excited!

（词数：49）

参考译文

一个阳光明媚的日子，尼克的爸爸和尼克一起做了一个风筝。他们用了一根竹竿、一些彩色的纸和一根长绳子。做完风筝后，他们把它带到公园去放飞。风筝在天空中飞得很高，像一只鸟。尼克太兴奋了!

考点锦囊

可数名词		用法	举例
动物	cat（猫）、dog（狗）、pig（猪）、horse（马）、cow（奶牛）、sheep（绵羊）	◆ 分单数和复数两种形式 ◆ 可数名词前可以用不定冠词、数词或some、many等修饰	a girl 一个女孩 an apple 一个苹果 some books 一些书
水果	apple（苹果）、banana（香蕉）、orange（橙子）、grape（葡萄）		
物品	book（书）、pen（钢笔）、chair（椅子）、table（桌子）、bag（包）、kite（风筝）、rope（绳子）		
人	boy（男孩）、girl（女孩）、man（男人）、woman（女人）、friend（朋友）		
*可数名词复数后面加-s还是-es，详情见"附录 可数名词复数变化规则"			

	不可数名词	用法	举例
物质名词	water（水）、milk（牛奶）、juice（果汁）、money（金钱）、bread（面包）、butter（黄油）、cheese（奶酪）、ice（冰）、meat（肉）、beef（牛肉）、chicken（鸡肉）、fish（鱼肉）、chalk（粉笔）、paper（纸）	◆ 没有复数形式 ◆ 前面不能用不定冠词、数词或many等词语修饰 ◆ 可以用some、a little、much、量词等修饰	some water 一些水 much food 一些食物 a piece of bread 一片面包
抽象名词	advice（建议）、fun（乐趣）、information（信息）、love（爱）、peace（和平）		
*可数名词和不可数名词，都可以用some修饰			

★必会句型★

1. 亲子活动

One sunny day, Nick's dad and Nick ... together. 在一个阳光明媚的日子，尼克的爸爸和尼克一起……

2. 风筝飞得高

The kite flew high in the sky, like a bird. 风筝在天空中飞得很高，像一只鸟。

Day 3　画画乐事

 考场模拟

Look at the three pictures.

Write the story shown in the pictures.

Write **35 words** or more.

思路点拨

Step 1:【审题】

弄清楚以下三点：

- 图片中的主要人物是谁，并给人物命名
- 图片中的名词有哪些
- 图片中的动词有哪些

Step 2:【描述3幅图片】

图1	名词	boy 男孩 paint 绘画颜料	picture 画 hand 手
	动词	is 是（过去式was）	get 使得（过去式got）
	组词成句	A **boy was painting** a **picture**. He **got the paints** all over his **hands**.	
图2	名词	sink 洗手池	
	动词	run 跑（过去式ran）	wash 洗（过去式washed）
	组词成句	He **ran** to the **sink** to **wash** hands.	
图3	名词	table 桌子	meal 一餐所吃的食物
	动词	sit 坐（过去式sat）　　sit down 坐下　　enjoy 享用（过去式enjoyed）	
	组词成句	The little boy **sat down** at the **table** to **enjoy** a **meal**.	

Step 3:【组句成段】

1. 故事开头：One day, ...

2. 故事发展：分别叙述三张图片

3. 故事结尾：After ...

Step 4:【检查修改】

☐ 1. 三幅图的要点描述全面　　　　☐ 2. 词数≥35

☐ 3. 使用过去时讲述故事　　　　☐ 4. 动词的过去式正确

☐ 5. 每个句子开头的首字母大写，名字首字母也大写

☐ 6. 每个句子末尾都要加上句号(.)

高分范文

One day, a little boy was joyfully painting a beautiful picture. Suddenly, he got the paints all over his hands by accident. Realizing his hands were dirty, he quickly ran to the sink to wash them carefully. After washing his hands, the little boy happily sat down at the table to enjoy a delicious meal.

（词数：55）

参考译文

有一天，一个小男孩正兴高采烈地画着一幅美丽的画。突然，他不小心把颜料弄得满手都是。意识到自己的手很脏，他赶紧跑到水池边仔细洗。洗手后，小男孩高兴地坐在桌边享用美味的饭菜。

考点锦囊

用形容词和副词丰富句子		
初始句子	One day, a boy was painting a picture.	☆☆
修改后的句子	One day, a **little** boy was **joyfully** painting a **beautiful** picture.	☆☆☆☆
初始句子	After washing his hands, the boy sat down at the table to enjoy a meal.	☆☆
修改后的句子	After washing his hands, the **little** boy **happily** sat down at the table to enjoy a **delicious** meal.	☆☆☆☆

描述人的形容词		
年龄	外貌	性格
young 年轻的	tall 高的	kind 善良的
old 年老的	short 矮的	friendly 友好的
middle-aged 中年的	thin 瘦的	outgoing 外向的

描述人的形容词		
年龄	外貌	性格
elderly 老年的	fat 胖的	shy 害羞的
adult 成年的	beautiful 漂亮的	polite 有礼貌的
little 小的	handsome 英俊的	impolite 无礼的
	pretty 可爱的	

副词		
well 好	easily 容易地	quietly 安静地
happily 高兴地	clearly 清晰地	noisily 吵闹地
joyfully 高兴地	carefully 仔细地	loudly 大声地
quickly 迅速地	busily 忙碌地	hungrily 饥饿地
fast 迅速地	angrily 生气地	

描述物的形容词		
味道	大小和年代	距离
delicious 美味的	tiny 极小的	long 长的
tasty 美味的	big 大的	short 短的
sweet 甜的	small 小的	far 远的
spicy 辛辣的	medium 中等的	close 接近的
salty 咸的	large 巨大的	near 近的
sour 酸的	modern 现代的	distant 遥远的
bitter 苦的	ancient 古代的	remote 偏远的

sit相关词组	
sit down 坐下	She **sat down** on the bed. 她在床上坐下。
sit out 耐心等到结束	They **sat out** the storm in a cafe. 他们坐在一家咖啡馆里，一直等到暴风雨过去。

★必会句型★

1. 故事开头

Once upon a time, a young boy was ... 从前，一个小男孩正……

2. 享受乐趣

The little boy happily enjoyed ... 小男孩高兴地享受着……

Day 4 购物小帮手

考场模拟

Look at the three pictures.

Write the story shown in the pictures.

Write **35 words** or more.

思路点拨

Step 1:【审题】

弄清楚以下三点:

- 图片中的主要人物是谁,并给人物命名
- 图片中的名词有哪些
- 图片中的动词有哪些

Step 2:【描述3幅图片】

图1	名词	Mark 马克 shopping list 购物清单	Mark's mother 马克的妈妈 money 钱
	动词	send 派（过去式sent） go shopping 去购物	give 给（过去式gave）
	组词成句	**Mark's mother sent** him to **go shopping.** She **gave** him a **shopping list** and some **money.**	

图2	名词	grocery store 杂货店 goods 商品；货品	shopping cart 购物车
	动词	go 去（过去式went） take 拿（过去式took）	enter 进入（过去式entered） put 放（过去式put）
	组词成句	Mark **went** to the **grocery store**. He **entered** the shop, **took** a **shopping cart**, and **put** the **goods** into the **cart**.	
图3	名词	checkout counter 结账柜台 change 找给的零钱	cashier 收银员
	动词	pay 付钱（过去式paid）	give 给（过去式gave）
	组词成句	Mark went to the **checkout counter**. He **paid** the money. A **cashier gave** him the **change**.	

Step 3:【组句成段】

　　1. 故事开头：On Saturday, ...

　　2. 故事发展：分别叙述三张图片

　　3. 故事结尾：Mark's mom was ...

Step 4:【检查修改】

　　□ 1. 三幅图的要点描述全面　　□ 2. 词数≥35

　　□ 3. 使用过去时讲述故事　　　□ 4. 动词的过去式正确

　　□ 5. 每个句子开头的首字母大写，名字首字母也大写

　　□ 6. 每个句子末尾都要加上句号(.)

📄 高分范文

　　On Saturday, Mark's mother sent him to go shopping. She gave him a shopping list and some money. So, Mark went to the nearest grocery store. He entered the shop, took a shopping cart, and put the goods into the cart. Then, Mark went to the checkout counter. After he paid the money, a cashier gave him the change. Mark's mom was very pleased with him and thanked him for being a great helper.

（词数：74）

参考译文

　　星期六，马克的妈妈叫他去购物。她给了他一张购物清单和一些钱。于是，马克去了最

近的杂货店。他走进商店，推了一辆购物车，把货物放进了购物车。然后，马克走到收银台。他付了钱后，收银员找给了他零钱。马克的妈妈对他很满意，并感谢他是个好帮手。

 考点锦囊

do sth. to sb. 相关搭配		
动词	搭配	举例
give 给	give sth. to sb. = give sb. sth. 把某物给某人	He **gave** Mike a ball as a gift. = He **gave** a ball to Mike as a gift. 他送给迈克一个球作为礼物。
*如果sb.是代词（me、him、her、them）时，只能用give sb. sth., 比如范文中的 "She gave him a shopping list and some money."		
show 展示	show sth. to sb. = show sb. sth. 向某人展示某物	**show** me the book = **show** the book **to** me 把书给我看看
pass 给；传递	pass sth. to sb. = pass sb. sth. 将某物传递给某人	**pass** me the ball = **pass** the ball **to** me 把球传给我

"购物用品" 相关表达	
名词及词组	动词及词组
shopping basket 购物篮	shop for 购买
shopping cart 购物车	check out 结账
receipt 收据	pay for 付款
price tag 价格标签	discount 打折
shopping list 购物清单	browse in the store 在商店里浏览
coupon 优惠券	compare prices 比较价格
loyalty card 会员卡	return goods 退货
gift card 礼品卡	exchange goods 换货
cashier 收银员	use coupons 使用优惠券
checkout counter 收银台	apply for a loyalty card 申请会员卡
change 找给的零钱	enter the shop 进商店

动词go构成的相关表达		
go + –ing	go for a +名词	go to the +名词
go hiking 去徒步旅行	go for a hike 去徒步旅行	go to the cinema 去看电影
go swimming 去游泳	go for a swim 去游泳	go to the concert 去参加音乐会
go skiing 去滑雪	go for a run 去跑步	go to the theatre 去剧院

续表

动词go构成的相关表达		
go + -ing	go for a +名词	go to the +名词
go camping 去野营	go for a walk 去散步	go to the opera 去剧院
go fishing 去钓鱼	go for a picnic 去野餐	go to the museum 去博物馆
go diving 去潜水	go for a jog 去慢跑	go to the gallery 去画廊
go boating 去划船	go for a ride 骑车兜风，骑马出游	go to the stadium 去体育场
go sightseeing 去观光	go for a drive 驱车兜风	go to the amusement park 去游乐园

★必会句型★

1. 分担家务

On Saturday, Mark's mother sent him to ... 星期六，马克的妈妈叫他……

2. 被表扬

Mark's ... was very pleased with him and thanked him for being a great helper. 马克的……对他很满意，并感谢他是个好帮手。

 Day 5　生日惊喜

 考场模拟

Look at the three pictures.

Write the story shown in the pictures.

Write **35 words** or more.

思路点拨

Step 1:【审题】

　　弄清楚以下三点：

- 图片中的主要人物是谁，并给人物命名
- 图片中的名词有哪些
- 图片中的动词有哪些

Step 2:【描述3幅图片】

图1	名词	birthday 生日 party 聚会 balloon 气球 birthday cake 生日蛋糕	my family and friends 我的家人和朋友 house 房子 streamer 装饰彩纸条
	动词	surprise 惊喜（过去式surprised） prepare 准备（过去式prepared）	decorate 装饰（过去式decorated）
	组词成句	On my last birthday, **my family** and **friends surprised** me with a magical **birthday party**. They **decorated** the **house** with **balloons** and **streamers**, and **prepared** a **birthday cake**.	
图2	名词	everyone 每人；所有人（代词，指代前面的my family and friends） door 门	
	动词	shout 喊（过去式shouted）	open 开（过去式opened）
	组词成句	I **opened the door**. **Everyone shouted** "Happy Birthday!".	
图3	名词	cake 蛋糕	
	动词	sing 唱（过去式sang）	eat 吃（过去式ate）
	组词成句	We **sang** and **ate cake** together.	

Step 3:【组句成段】

1. 故事开头：On my last birthday, ...

2. 故事发展：分别叙述三张图片

3. 故事结尾：I will always remember ...

Step 4:【检查修改】

☐ 1. 三幅图的要点描述全面   ☐ 2. 词数≥35

☐ 3. 使用过去时讲述故事   ☐ 4. 动词的过去式正确

☐ 5. 每个句子开头的首字母大写，名字首字母也大写

☐ 6. 每个句子末尾都要加上句号(.)

📄 高分范文

On my last birthday, my family and friends surprised me with a magical birthday party. They decorated the house with balloons and streamers, and prepared a delicious birthday cake. When I opened the door, everyone shouted "Happy Birthday!" and I was so happy! We had a great time singing and eating cake together. I will always remember this special birthday.

（词数：60）

参考译文

在我的上一个生日，我的家人和朋友给了我一个惊喜，一个神奇的生日聚会。他们用气球和彩带装饰了房子，并准备了一个美味的生日蛋糕。当我打开门的时候，每个人都喊着"生日快乐！"我很高兴！我们在一起唱歌和吃蛋糕玩得很开心。我将永远记住这个特别的生日。

考点锦囊

A2 Key中既是动词又是形容词的词汇		
open	v. 打开	I **opened** the door. 我打开了门。
	adj. 开着的	The door is **open**. 门是开着的。
close	v. 关，关闭	She **closed** the book. 她合上了书。
	adj. 关闭的	The door is **closed**. 门是关着的。
clean	v. 打扫	Ellen cooked and **cleaned** for them. 艾伦为他们做饭、打扫卫生。
	adj. 干净的	The house was **clean** and tidy after cleaning. 打扫后的房子又干净又整洁。
tidy	v. 使整洁	I spent all morning cleaning and **tidying**. 我用了整个上午的时间清扫整理。
	adj. 整洁的	She keeps her flat very **tidy**. 她把她的单元房间保持得很整洁。
dry	v. 使变干	I towelled myself **dry**. 我用毛巾把自己擦干。
	adj. 干的	The ground is **dry** after a long period without rain. 经过长时间不下雨，地面变得干燥了。

"生日派对" 相关表达	
名词及词组	动词及词组
birthday party 生日聚会	light the candles 点燃蜡烛
birthday cake 生日蛋糕	sing the birthday song 唱生日快乐歌
birthday candle 生日蜡烛	blow out the candles 吹灭蜡烛
birthday present 生日礼物	make a wish 许愿
birthday card 生日卡片	eat the cake 吃蛋糕
balloon 气球	open the presents 拆礼物
streamer 装饰彩纸条	thank the giver 感谢送礼的人
a bunch of flowers 一束花	cut the cake 切蛋糕
gift box 礼物盒	enjoy the party 享受聚会
birthday hat 生日帽子	

★必会句型★

1. 惊喜

My family and friends surprised me ... 我的家人和朋友给了我一个惊喜……

2. 铭记在心

I will always remember this day. 我将永远记住这个日子。

Weekend 二 每周一练

I. 写出下列动词的过去式。

1. enjoy _____   7. pay _____

2. enter _____   8. send _____

3. fly _____   9. take _____

4. get _____   10. walk _____

5. give _____   11. wash _____

6. keep _____   12. win _____

II. 读一读，圈出正确的单词。

1. There is a roast chicken sand some **egg / eggs**.

2. We stopped and bought some **breads / bread**.

3. She found the fox and gave some **water / waters** to him.

4. We haven't got **some / any** lemonade.

5. There is some **milk / milks** in the fridge.

6. She eats a lot of **chocolate / chocolates**.

7. He lost all his **money / moneys**.

8. There's **a / some** cat in the garden.

III. 选词填空。

| jumped | called | had | ate | threw | sang |

1. A woman _____ my name loudly.

2. He _____ the key onto the table.

3. Everybody _____ a good time.

4. The boy _____ onto her bike and rode away!

5. The children _____ their pizzas hungrily.

6. She _____ the song beautifully!

IV. 将左右两列的相应内容连线，构成完整的一句话。

1. It's Mike's birthday   A. and a cup of juice.

2. Emma went to a bookstore   B. it was already 10 a.m.

3. When he woke up   C. to find some books to read.

4. Jim was very hungry   D. watch a film at home.

5. He ordered a piece of bread   E. and he is really happy.

6. She decided to invite Ellen to   F. and he went to the kitchen.

V. 判断下面句子正误，如有错，请圈出并将正确形式写在下面的横线上。

1. Mark doesn't sleep well last night.   ☐

_____

2. Max ate a big slice, and it was fantastic! ☐

_____

3. One day, a boy was walking to school and it starts to rain. ☐

_____

4. She closed the door quiet. ☐

_____

5. We only have some waters in the fridge. ☐

_____

6. The boys ate everything on the table. ☐

_____

VI. 连词成句。

1. He, look, at, his, didn't, clock.

_____

2. The, weather, great, at, was, the, weekend.

_____

3. warm, It, was, and, sunny.

_____

4. thunderstorm, I, heard, the, last, night.

_____

5. centre, Max, was, in, the, city, with, his, mum.

_____

6. He, play, decided, to, football.

_____

7. decided, to, Martin, make, a, cake.

_____

8. She, to, the, supermarket, went, to, buy, some, eggs.

_____

看图作文：假期游玩

		第7周目标		
考试模块	时间	主题	内容	
	Day 1	动物园之旅	On Saturday, Lily went to the zoo with her mum and dad.	☐
	Day 2	海边度假	On a sunny day, Mike and his father took a walk along the beach.	☐
Part 7 看图作文	Day 3	班级旅行	Yesterday, Tom visited the nature museum with his classmates.	☐
	Day 4	雨后出游	One day, a family was getting ready to go on vacation.	☐
	Day 5	公园游玩	In the park, a girl was playing with her friends.	☐
	Weekend	每周一练	基础练习	☐

Day 1　动物园之旅

 考场模拟

Look at the three pictures.

Write the story shown in the pictures.

Write **35 words** or more.

 思路点拨

Step 1:【审题】

　　弄清楚以下三点：

- 图片中的主要人物是谁，并给人物命名
- 图片中的名词有哪些
- 图片中的动词有哪些

Step 2:【描述3幅图片】

图1	名词	Lily 莉莉 sandwich 三明治 camera 相机	mum and dad 妈妈和爸爸（=parents） zoo 动物园
	动词	go 去（过去式went）	bring 带（过去式brought）
	组词成句	**Lily went** to the **zoo** with her **mum and dad**. Mom **brought sandwiches** for lunch. Dad **brought** the **camera**.	
图2	名词	giraffe 长颈鹿	
	动词	go 去（过去式went） took photos 拍照片	take 拿（过去式took）
	组词成句	They **went** to see the **giraffes**. Lily's dad **took photos**.	
图3	名词	monkey 猴子	tree 树
	动词	go 去（过去式went） swing 摇晃（现在分词swinging）	are 是（过去式were）
	组词成句	They **went** to see the **monkeys**. **Monkeys were swinging** between **trees**.	

Step 3:【组句成段】

1. 故事开头：On a sunny Saturday, ...

2. 故事发展：分别叙述三张图片

3. 故事结尾：She had a really great day ...

Step 4:【检查修改】

☐ 1. 三幅图的要点描述全面　　　☐ 2. 词数≥35

□ 3. 使用过去时讲述故事　　　□ 4. 动词的过去式正确

□ 5. 每个句子开头的首字母大写，名字首字母也大写

□ 6. 每个句子末尾都要加上句号(.)

📄 高分范文

On Saturday, Lily went to the zoo with her mum and dad. Mum brought sandwiches for lunch, and dad brought the camera. They went to see the giraffes first and Lily's dad took some photos. Then, they went to see the monkeys which were swinging between trees. Lily thought the monkeys were very funny. She had a really great day with her parents.

（词数：63）

参考译文

　　星期六，莉莉和妈妈爸爸一起去了动物园。妈妈带了三明治当午餐，爸爸带了相机。他们先去看了长颈鹿，莉莉的爸爸拍了一些照片。然后，他们去看猴子，它们在树间荡来荡去。莉莉觉得猴子很有趣。她和父母度过了美好的一天。

🔔 考点锦囊

时间介词in / on / at			
in	一天中的某个阶段	**in** the morning 在早上 **in** the evening 在傍晚	**in** the afternoon 在下午
	月份、季节	**in** February 在二月 **in** spring 在春天 **in** autumn 在秋天	**in** September 在九月 **in** summer 在夏天 **in** winter 在冬天
	年份	**in** 2024 在2024年	
	其他词组	**in** three hours 3个小时后	
on	一周中的某天	**on** Monday 在周一 **on** a sunny Monday 在一个晴朗的周一	
	日期	**on** 18th August 在8月18日	**on** 3rd May 在5月3日
	一些节假日	**on** New Year's Day 在元旦	
at	时刻（o'clock）	**at** 7 o'clock 在7点钟	**at** 7 a.m. 在早上7点
	weekend和night	**at** the weekend 在周末	**at** night 在晚上
	用餐时间	**at** lunchtime 在午餐时间	

★ *必会句型* ★

1. 亲子活动

On Saturday, Lily went to ... with her mum and dad. 星期六，莉莉和妈妈爸爸一起去了……

2. 美好一天

She had a really great day with ... 她和……度过了美好的一天。

Day 2　海边度假

 考场模拟

Look at the three pictures.

Write the story shown in the pictures.

Write **35 words** or more.

 思路点拨

Step 1：【审题】

弄清楚以下三点：

- 图片中的主要人物是谁，并给人物命名
- 图片中的名词有哪些
- 图片中的动词有哪些

Step 2:【描述3幅图片】

图1	名词	Mike 迈克 walk 散步	father 爸爸 beach 海滩
	动词	take 拿（过去式took）	take a walk 散步
	组词成句	**Mike** and his **father took a walk** along the **beach**.	
图2	名词	shell 贝壳 sand castle 沙堡	bucket 桶
	动词	collect 收集（过去式collected）	build 建造（过去式built）
	组词成句	They **collected shells** in a **bucket**. They **built** a **sand castle**.	
图3	名词	water 水	
	动词	go 去（过去式went）	play 玩（过去式played）
	组词成句	They **went** swimming together and **played** in the **water**.	

Step 3:【组句成段】

1. 故事开头：On a sunny day, ...

2. 故事发展：分别叙述三张图片

3. 故事结尾：The boy and his father had a fun day ...

Step 4:【检查修改】

□ 1. 三幅图的要点描述全面 　　□ 2. 词数≥35

□ 3. 使用过去时讲述故事 　　□ 4. 动词的过去式正确

□ 5. 每个句子开头的首字母大写，名字首字母也大写

□ 6. 每个句子末尾都要加上句号(.)

📄 高分范文

　　On a sunny day, Mike and his father took a walk along the beach. They collected shells in a bucket and built a huge sand castle. Then, they went swimming together and played in the water. The boy and his father had a fun day at the beach!

（词数：48）

参考译文

　　在一个阳光明媚的日子，迈克和他的父亲沿着海滩散步。他们收集贝壳放在一个桶里并建了一个巨大的沙堡。然后，他们一起去游泳，在水里玩耍。男孩和他的父亲在海滩上度过了愉快的一天！

 ## 考点锦囊

"户外活动"相关表达		
名词及词组	**动词词组**	**介词词组**
campsite 露营地	put up tents 搭帐篷	at the campsite 在露营地
tent 帐篷	pitch a tent 搭帐篷	by the campfire 在篝火旁
sleeping bag 睡袋	make camp 帐篷	in the tent 在帐篷里
backpack 背包	sleep in a sleeping bag 在睡袋里睡觉	with the camper 和露营者一起
campfire 篝火	cook on a campfire 在篝火上烹饪	around the fire 在火堆周围
barbecue 烧烤	have a barbecue 烧烤	under the stars 在星空下
first-aid kit 急救箱	hike in the woods 在树林里徒步旅行	
flashlight 手电筒	explore the nature 探索大自然	
match 火柴	have fun in the outdoors 在户外娱乐	
camper 露营者	collect seashells 捡贝壳	
summer camp 夏令营	play with sand 玩沙子	

人称代词	单数		复数	
	主格	**宾格**	**主格**	**宾格**
第一人称	I 我	me	we 我们	us
第二人称	you 你	you	you 你们	you
第三人称	he 他	him	they 他/她/它们	them
	she 她	her		
	it 它	it		
用法	主格：作主语			
	宾格：作动词或介词宾语			
	*图片主要人物为a girl、a woman时，主语可用人称代词she替换； 图片主要人物为a boy、a man时，主语可用人称代词he替换； 图片主要人物为"第三人称多个人"时，主语可用人称代词they替换			

物主代词	单数		复数	
	形容词性	名词性	形容词性	名词性
第一人称	my 我的	mine	our 我们的	ours
第二人称	your 你的	yours	your 你们的	yours
第三人称	his 他的	his	their 他/她/它们的	theirs
	her 她的	hers		
	its 它的	its		

★必会句型★

1. 海边散步

On a sunny day, Mike and his ... took a walk along the beach. 在一个阳光明媚的日子，迈克和他的……沿着海滩散步。

2. 美好一天

The boy and his ... had a fun day at the beach! 男孩和他的……在海滩上度过了愉快的一天！

Day 3　班级旅行

考场模拟

Look at the three pictures.

Write the story shown in the pictures.

Write **35 words** or more.

思路点拨

Step 1:【审题】

弄清楚以下三点：

- 图片中的主要人物是谁，并给人物命名
- 图片中的名词有哪些
- 图片中的动词有哪些

Step 2:【描述3幅图片】

图1	名词	Tom 汤姆 bus 公交车	classmate 同班同学 by bus 乘公交车	7 a.m. 早上7点
	动词	visit 参观（过去式visited）	go 去（过去式went）	
	组词成句	**Tom visited** the nature museum with his **classmates.** They **went** to the museum **by bus** at **7 a.m.**		
图2	名词	museum 博物馆 dinosaur skeleton 恐龙骨架	display 展览品 ancient animal 古代动物	
	动词	arrive 到达（过去式arrived）	see 看见（过去式saw）	
	组词成句	They **arrived** the **museum.** They **saw** many **displays**, such as **dinosaur skeletons** and **ancient animals.**		
图3	名词	dinosaur 恐龙	robot 机器人	
	动词	hear 听见（过去式heard） come to life 活过来	turn 转（过去式turned）	
	组词成句	He **heard** a noise and **turned** to see a **dinosaur** "**come to life**"! It was just a **robot.**		

Step 3:【组句成段】

1. 故事开头：Yesterday, Tom visited ...

2. 故事发展：分别叙述三张图片

3. 故事结尾：Tom couldn't wait to tell his parents about the trip!

Step 4:【检查修改】

☐ 1. 三幅图的要点描述全面　　　☐ 2. 词数≥35

☐ 3. 使用过去时讲述故事　　　☐ 4. 动词的过去式正确

☐ 5. 每个句子开头的首字母大写，名字首字母也大写

☐ 6. 每个句子末尾都要加上句号(.)

📄 高分范文

Yesterday, Tom visited the nature museum with his classmates. They went to the museum by bus at 7 a.m.. After they arrived the museum, they saw many interesting displays, such as dinosaur skeletons and ancient animals. Suddenly, he heard a noise and turned to see a dinosaur "come to life"! But it was just a robot. Tom couldn't wait to tell his parents about the trip!

（词数：66）

参考译文

昨天，汤姆和他的同学参观了自然博物馆。早上7点，他们乘公共汽车去了博物馆。到达博物馆后，他们看到了许多有趣的展品，比如恐龙骨架和古代动物。突然，他听到一声巨响，转身看到一只恐龙"活过来了"！但它只是一个机器人。汤姆迫不及待地想把这次旅行告诉他的父母！

考点锦囊

常用-ed形容词和-ing形容词	
-ed形容词	-ing形容词
interested 感兴趣的	interesting 有趣的
excited 激动的	exciting 令人兴奋的
pleased 高兴的	pleasing 令人高兴的
surprised 吃惊的	surprising 令人感到惊讶的
tired 累的	tiring 累人的
bored 无聊的	boring 令人感到乏味的
moved 感动的	moving 动人的
worried 担心的	worrying 令人担心的
frightened 恐惧的	frightening 可怕的

续表

常用-ed形容词和-ing形容词	
-ed形容词	-ing形容词
disappointed 失望的	disappointing 令人失望的
*-ed形容词用于形容人；-ing形容词用于形容物	

turn相关词组	
turn off 关闭	Please **turn** the television **off** before you go to bed. 睡觉前请关上电视。
turn on 打开	I'll **turn** the television **on**. 我来打开电视机。
turn back 原路返回	The weather became so bad that they had to **turn back**. 天气变得非常恶劣，他们不得不按原路折回。
turn down 开小，调低	He **turned** the lights **down** low. 他把灯光调得暗了一些。
turn up 开大，调高	The music was **turned up** loud. 音乐的音量开大了。

★必会句型★

1. **班级旅行**

   Yesterday, Tom visited ... with his classmates. 昨天，汤姆和他的同学参观了……

2. **期待分享**

   Tom couldn't wait to tell his ... about the trip! 汤姆迫不及待地想把这次旅行告诉他的……

Day 4　雨后出游

 考场模拟

Look at the three pictures.

Write the story shown in the pictures.

Write **35 words** or more.

思路点拨

Step 1:【审题】

弄清楚以下三点：

- 图片中的主要人物是谁，并给人物命名
- 图片中的名词有哪些
- 图片中的动词有哪些

Step 2:【描述3幅图片】

图1	名词	family 家人	rainstorm 暴风雨
	动词	are 是（过去式were） go on vacation 去度假 be about to 即将要做	hit 撞（过去式hit） get ready 准备好
	组词成句	A **family** was **getting ready** to **go on vacation**. They **were about to** leave. A sudden **rainstorm hit**.	
图2	名词	rain 雨	house 房子
	动词	decide 决定（过去式decided）	watch 看（过去式watched）
	组词成句	They **decided** to wait it out and **watched** the rain from inside the house.	
图3	名词	sun 太阳	
	动词	come 来（过去式came） come out（太阳、星星或月亮）出来	continue 继续（过去式continued）
	组词成句	The **sun came out**. They **continued** to **drive**.	

Step 3:【组句成段】

1. 故事开头：One day, ...

2. 故事发展：分别叙述三张图片

3. 故事结尾：They had a good holiday ...

Step 4:【检查修改】

- □ 1. 三幅图的要点描述全面
- □ 2. 词数≥35
- □ 3. 使用过去时讲述故事
- □ 4. 动词的过去式正确
- □ 5. 每个句子开头的首字母大写，名字首字母也大写
- □ 6. 每个句子末尾都要加上句号(.)

高分范文

One day, a family was getting ready to go on vacation. However, as they were about to leave, a sudden rainstorm hit. They decided to wait it out and watched the rain from inside the house. An hour later, the sun came out and they happily continued to drive. They had a good holiday despite the rain.

（词数：57）

参考译文

一天，一家人正准备去度假。然而，就在他们准备离开的时候，突然下起了暴雨。他们决定等雨停，然后在屋里看雨。一小时后，太阳出来了，他们高兴地继续开车。尽管下雨，他们的假期过得很愉快。

考点锦囊

"动词+to do" 用法		
agree to do 同意做	manage to do 设法做	want to do 想要做
ask to do 请求做	promise to do 承诺做	wish to do 希望做
get ready to do 准备做	plan to do 计划做	hope to do 希望做
decide to do 决定做	prefer to do 更喜欢做	start to do 开始做

A2 Key中既是副词又是介词的词汇		
inside	*adv.* 在里面	We had to move **inside** when it started to rain. 开始下雨了，我们只好躲进屋里。
inside	*prep.* 在……内	Go **inside** the house. 进屋里吧。
across	*adv.* 横过	He walked **across** the bridge. 他走过桥。
across	*prep.* 在……对面	There's a bank right **across** the street. 街对面就有一家银行。

A2 Key中既是副词又是介词的词汇		
around	*adv.* 到处	travel **around** 周游旅行
	prep. 围绕	sit **around** the table 围坐在桌子旁
about	*adv.* 大约	I have **about** £3. 我大约有3英镑。
	prep. 关于	a book **about** animals 一本关于动物的书
* *adv.* 是副词，*prep.* 是介词； 副词，多放在动词后面，或be动词、助动词或情态动词之后，实义动词之前； 介词，用于名词或者代词的前面		

as相关词组	
the same as 与……相同	His opinion is **the same as** mine. 他的观点与我的相同。
as good as 与……一样好	His English is **as good as** mine. 他的英语跟我的英语一样好。
as soon as possible 尽快	We'll get back to you **as soon as possible**. 我们将尽快再跟你联系。
as well 也	I'll have a cup of coffee **as well**. 我也要一杯咖啡。
as well as 还	She is good at singing **as well as** dancing. 她不仅擅长唱歌，还擅长跳舞。

★必会句型★

1. 准备度假

One day, ... was / were getting ready to go on vacation. 一天，……正准备去度假。

2. 意外暴雨

However, as they were about to ..., a sudden rainstorm hit. 然而，就在他们准备……的时候，突然下起了暴雨。

Day 5　公园游玩

考场模拟

Look at the three pictures.

Write the story shown in the pictures.

Write **35 words** or more.

 思路点拨

Step 1:【审题】

弄清楚以下三点：

- 图片中的主要人物是谁，并给人物命名
- 图片中的名词有哪些
- 图片中的动词有哪些

Step 2:【描述3幅图片】

图1	名词	girl 女孩 park 公园 goldfish 金鱼	her friend 她的朋友 lake 湖
	动词	is 是（过去式was） play 玩（现在分词playing）	are 是（过去式were）
	组词成句	In the park, a girl **was playing** with **her friends**. There were some **goldfish** in the **lake**.	
图2	名词	water 水	ground 地；地面
	动词	jump 跳（过去式jumped）	land 着陆（过去式landed）
	组词成句	One of the goldfish **jumped** out of the **water** and **landed** on the **ground**.	
图3	名词	girl 女孩	her two friends 她的两个朋友
	动词	put back 将……放回	
	组词成句	**The girl** and **her two friends** together **put** the goldfish **back** into the water.	

Step 3:【组句成段】

1. 故事开头：In the park, ...

2. 故事发展：分别叙述三张图片

3. 故事结尾：They were very ...

Step 4:【检查修改】

☐ 1. 三幅图的要点描述全面　　☐ 2. 词数≥35

☐ 3. 使用过去时讲述故事　　☐ 4. 动词的过去式正确

☐ 5. 每个句子开头的首字母大写，名字首字母也大写

☐ 6. 每个句子末尾都要加上句号(.)

📄 高分范文

In the park, a girl was playing with her friends. There were some goldfish in the lake. Suddenly, one of the goldfish jumped out of the water and landed on the ground. The girl and her two friends put the goldfish back into the water together. They were very happy to help the little fish return to its home.

（词数：59）

参考译文

在公园里，一个女孩正在和她的朋友们玩。湖里有许多金鱼。突然，其中一条金鱼跳出水面，落在地上。女孩和她的两个朋友一起把金鱼放回水里。他们非常高兴帮助小鱼回到了它的家。

🔔 考点锦囊

There be句型	
There is + 可数名词单数 / 不可数名词 + 地点状语	**There is** an apple in the fridge. 冰箱里有一个苹果。
There are + 可数名词复数 + 地点状语	**There are** many people in the park. 公园里有很多人。

put相关词组	
put back 将……放回	She stopped and **put back** the strawberry again. 她停下来，把草莓放回原处。
put on 穿上，上演	She **put on** her coat and went out. 她穿上外套，出去了。

续表

put相关词组	
put off 脱掉	He **put off** his wet clothes and put on a dry towel. 他脱掉湿衣服，换上了一条干毛巾。
put up 张贴，搭建	They **put up** a tent for the night. 他们支起帐篷过夜。
put out 扑灭	The firemen are trying to **put out** the fire. 消防队员正在设法扑灭大火。
put in 提交	Please **put in** your homework on time. 请按时交作业。
put sth. away 将某物收好	I always **put away** my clothes after I wear them. 我总是在穿过衣服后把它们收起来。

★必会句型★

1. 公园玩耍

In the park, a girl was playing with her ... 在公园里，一个女孩正在和她的……玩耍。

2. 提供帮助

They were very happy to help ... 他们非常高兴地帮助……

Weekend 二 每周一练

I. 写出下列动词的过去式。

1. are _____

2. arrive _____

3. bring _____

4. collect _____

5. decide _____

6. build _____

7. hear _____

8. jump _____

9. play _____

10. turn _____

11. visit _____

12. watch _____

II. 读一读，圈出正确的单词。

1. I wanted to buy some **new / slow** coat.

2. Tom was feeling **happy / tall**.

3. The cashier was very **polite / empty**.

4. The city was quite **busy / pleased**.

5. He's very **interested / interesting** in history.

6. It was a **great / high** film.

7. The boy was carrying a **small / ready** suitcase.

8. They had a **wonderful / careful** time!

III. 选词填空。

| run | raining | listening | eaten | lived | watching |

1. It was _____ a lot.

2. Lily was _____ a film when she heard a strange noise.

3. I'm tired because I've just _____ a race.

4. My brother hasn't _____ his lunch because he's sick.

5. When my mom got home, I was _____ to music.

6. I've _____ in my house for a long time.

IV. 将左右两列的相应内容连线，构成完整的一句话。

1. Her mother bought two tickets   A. together in the gym.

2. Tom invited him to take exercise   B. from the ticket office.

3. It was too expensive   C. her luggage in the bedroom.

4. Jessie was packing   D. for her to afford.

5. He hurried to the bus stop   E. covered in snow.

6. Everything outdoors was   F. but failed to catch it.

V. 判断下面句子正误，如有错，请圈出并将正确形式写在下面的横线上。

1. Yesterday, I visit my sick grandfather.   ☐

_____

2. She opened the letter slow.   ☐

_____

3. I quick read the letter.   ☐

_____

4. There are a lot of food on the table.   ☐

_____

5. My house has seven room.   ☐

_____

6. They built a snow dog and gave it a scarf.   ☐

_____

VI. 连词成句。

1. He cycled in the park.

   He saw Alice.   (when)

   _____

2. It was John's birthday.

   He and his parents went to his favourite restaurant.   (so)

   _____

3. David wasn't late.

   His mum gave him a lift.   (because)

   _____

4. They were all very hungry.

   They ordered two pizzas on the menu.   (so)

   _____

5. I put my pen back in my bag.

   I found it.   (after)

   _____

6. I was fishing yesterday.

   I met a really interesting person.   (when)

   _____

7. He was happy.

   It was a sunny day.   (because)

   _____

8. Bob arrived at the park.

   He saw that many people were already there.   (after)

   _____

Week 8 考试全流程模拟练习

第8周目标			
考试模块	时间	主题	
考试全流程模拟练习	Day 1	邮件写作	☐
	Day 2	邮件写作 高分范文	☐
	Day 3	看图作文	☐
	Day 4	看图作文 高分范文	☐
	Day 5	邮件写作和看图作文 必会句型	☐

Day 1 邮件写作

 考场模拟

You didn't go to your friend's birthday party last night.

Write a note to your friend, Ann:

- explain why you didn't go

- tell her when and where you can meet her

Write **25 words** or more.

 思路点拨

Step 1:【审题，划重点】

弄清楚以下三点：

- 便条写给谁

- 写便条的原因

- 要回答的三个问题

Step 2:【回答三个问题】

回答问题	why 为什么	
	when 什么时候	
	where 在哪里	

Step 3:【组句成段】

1. 表明便条目的

2. 回答三个问题

3. 结尾语

Step 4:【检查修改】

□ 1. 开头称呼和结束语正确　　□ 2. 回答了3个问题

□ 3. 词数≥25　　　　　　　　□ 4. 无拼写错误

□ 5. 无语法错误

Day 2　邮件写作 高分范文

Step 1:【审题，划重点】

弄清楚以下三点：

- 便条写给谁

- 写便条的原因

- 要回答的三个问题

You didn't go to your friend's birthday party last night. —— 写便条的目的

Write a note to your friend, Ann: —— 要给她写便条

- explain **why** you didn't go

- tell her **when** and **where** you can meet her —— 要回答的3个问题

Write **25 words** or more.

Step 2:【回答三个问题】

回答问题	why 为什么	not feel well 感觉不舒服
		I'm sorry ... because ... 我很抱歉……，因为……
	when 什么时候	this Saturday 本周六
		Would you like to ...? 你愿意……吗?
	where 在哪里	at the cinema 在电影院
		We can ... 我们可以……

Step 3:【组句成段】

1. 表明便条目的：I'm sorry ...

2. 回答三个问题

3. 结尾语：Best wishes,

Step 4:【检查修改】

☐ 1. 开头称呼和结束语正确　　☐ 2. 回答了3个问题

☐ 3. 词数≥25　　☐ 4. 无拼写错误

☐ 5. 无语法错误

📄 高分范文

Hi Ann,

I'm sorry I didn't go to your birthday party because I didn't feel well last night. Would you like to meet this Saturday? We can watch a movie together at the cinema. Hope to see you.

Best wishes,

Sally

（词数：40）

参考译文

嗨，安：

我很抱歉没有去参加你的生日聚会，因为我昨晚感觉不舒服。你想这个星期六见个面吗？我们可以一起在电影院看一场电影。希望能见到你。

祝好

莎莉

Day 3　看图作文

 考场模拟

Look at the three pictures.

Write the story shown in the pictures.

Write **35 words** or more.

 思路点拨

Step 1:【审题】

弄清楚以下三点：

• 图片中的主要人物是谁，并给人物命名

• 图片中的名词有哪些

• 图片中的动词有哪些

Step 2:【描述3幅图片】

图1	名词	
	动词	
	组词成句	
图2	名词	
	动词	
	组词成句	
图3	名词	
	动词	
	组词成句	

Step 3:【组句成段】

    1. 故事开头

    2. 故事发展：分别叙述三张图片

    3. 故事结尾

Step 4:【检查修改】

□ 1. 三幅图的要点描述全面   □ 2. 词数≥35

□ 3. 使用过去时讲述故事   □ 4. 动词的过去式正确

□ 5. 每个句子开头的首字母大写，名字首字母也大写

□ 6. 每个句子末尾都要加上句号(.)

Day 4   看图作文 高分范文

Step 1:【审题】

弄清楚以下三点：

- 图片中的主要人物是谁，并给人物命名

- 图片中的名词有哪些

- 图片中的动词有哪些

Week 8

Step 2:【描述3幅图片】

图1	名词	Emma 艾玛 toy store 玩具店	her mother 她的妈妈
	动词	go 去（过去式went）	
	组词成句	**Emma** and **her mother went** to the **toy store**.	
图2	名词	toy 玩具	brown bear 棕色的熊
	动词	look 看（过去式looked） buy 买（过去式bought）	love 爱（过去式loved）
	组词成句	They **looked** at the **toys**. Emma **loved** a **brown bear** and **bought** it.	
图3	名词	gift box 礼物盒 gift 礼物	friend 朋友 Kate 凯特
	动词	give 给（过去式gave）	receive 收到（过去式received）
	组词成句	Emma **gave** the **gift box** to her **friend** Kate. Kate was very happy when she **received** the **gift**.	

Step 3:【组句成段】

1. 故事开头：Emma and her mother ...

2. 故事发展：分别叙述三张图片

3. 故事结尾：Kate was very ...

Step 4:【检查修改】

□ 1. 三幅图的要点描述全面　　□ 2. 词数≥35

□ 3. 使用过去时讲述故事　　□ 4. 动词的过去式正确

□ 5. 每个句子开头的首字母大写，名字首字母也大写

□ 6. 每个句子末尾都要加上句号(.)

138

高分范文

Emma and her mother went to the toy store. They looked at the toys. Emma loved a brown bear and bought it. The next day, Emma gave the gift box to her friend Kate because it was her birthday. Kate was very happy when she received the gift.

（词数：48）

参考译文

艾玛和妈妈去了玩具店。她们看了看玩具。艾玛喜欢一只棕熊，然后买下了它。第二天，艾玛把礼盒送给了她的朋友凯特，因为那天是她的生日。凯特收到礼物时非常高兴。

Day 5　邮件写作和看图作文 必会句型

一、邮件写作七类必会句型

A2 Key Part 6写作考试中，需要掌握的句型有七类：分享和推荐、提议或计划、表示邀请、表达歉意、表达感谢、请求帮助和委婉表达。

1. 分享和推荐

1) **I wanted to share ... with you.** 我想和你分享……

I want to share my holiday **with you.** 我想和你分享我的假期。

2) **I wanted to tell you ...** 我想告诉你……

I wanted to tell you about the picnic. 我想告诉你野餐的事。

3) **I would like to recommend ...** 我想推荐……

I would like to recommend the Chinese cuisine in that restaurant. 我想推荐一下那家餐厅的中国菜。

4) **My favourite ... is ...** 我最喜欢的……是……

My favourite food **is** dumpling. 我最喜欢的食物是饺子。

2. 提议或计划

1) **Why don't we ...?** 我们为什么不……呢？

Why don't we go and see it together? 咱们为什么不一起去看看呢？

2) **How about ...?/ What about ...?** ……怎么样？

How about we meet at the bus station? 我们在公交车站见面怎么样？

3) **Let's ...** 让我们……

Let's go fishing this weekend. 咱们这个周末去钓鱼吧。

4) **Could you bring ...?** 你能带……吗？

By the way, **could you please bring** some bread? 顺便问一下，你能带一些面包吗？

5) **Don't forget ...** 别忘了……

Don't forget to wear comfortable shoes. 别忘了穿舒适的鞋。

6) **You can bring ...** 你可以带……

You can bring some snacks and water. 你可以带一些零食和水。

3. 表示邀请

1) **Would you like to ...?** 你想……吗？

Would you like to come with me? 你愿意和我一起去吗？

2) **Do you want to ...?** 你想……吗？

Do you want to go to the sports centre? 你想去体育中心吗？

4. 表达歉意

1) **I'm afraid that I can't ...** 恐怕我不能……

I'm afraid that I can't go skiing with you next weekend.

恐怕下周末我不能和你一起去滑雪了。

2) **I'm sorry, but I can't ...** 很抱歉，但我不能……

I'm sorry, but I can't go to the park with you on Sunday.

很抱歉，我周日不能和你一起去公园了。

3) **I'd love to ..., but ...** 我很想……，但……

I'd love to go shopping with you, **but I will not be able to come**.

我很想和你一起去购物，但是我不能来了。

4) **I can't go, because ...** 我去不了，因为……

I can't go because I have much homework to do. 我去不了，因为我有许多作业要做。

5) **I'm supposed to go, but ...** 我本打算去的，但是……

I'm supposed to go, but I have an exam next week. 我本打算去的，但是下周我有一个考试。

5. 表达感谢

1) **Thank you so much for ...** 非常感谢……

Thank you so much for being my guide. 非常感谢你做我的导游。

2) **I really appreciate ...** 我真的很感激……

I really appreciate that you lent me fifty yuan. 我真的很感激你借给我50元。

6. 请求帮助

1) **Could you please ...** 你可以……吗?

Could you please help me with my homework? 你能帮我完成我的家庭作业吗?

2) **Is it OK if I ...?** 我……，行吗?

Is it OK if I borrow the book? 我借这本书，行吗?

7. 委婉表达

May I kindly ...? 我可以……吗?

May I kindly request a day off today? 我明天可以请一天假吗?

二、看图写作二类必会句型

A2 Key Part 7写作考试中，需要掌握的句型有两类：故事开头和故事结尾。

1. 故事开头：描述性总结

1) **It was ...** 那（天）是……

It was a sunny day. 那是一个阳光明媚的一天。

2) **Yesterday, ...** 昨天，……

Yesterday, she went to the zoo with her mother. 昨天，她和妈妈去了动物园。

3) **One day, ...** 一天……

One day, his family and he had a picnic. 一天，他的家人和他去野餐。

2. 故事结尾：心情描述

1) **She was very ...** 她非常……

She was very happy. 她非常高兴。

2) **He felt ...** 他感到……

He felt very lucky. 他感到非常幸运。

3) **They had a ... time.** 他们玩得很……

They had a good **time.** 他们玩得很开心。

4) **What a ...!** 多么……！

What a nice day! 多么愉快的一天啊！

参考答案

Week 2 每周一练

I 1. at   2. in   3. on   4. at   5. in   6. on

II 1. need   2. lend   3. meet   4. grateful   5. go   6. forget

III 1. B   2. A   3. D   4. C   5. F   6. E

IV
1. It's a funny film.

2. I knew I had made a big mistake.

3. I don't know the city well.

4. We had lunch in a small restaurant.

5. He likes to eat a lot of chocolate.

6. Can you tell me a cheap store?

7. A kind girl showed me the way to the bus stop.

8. I haven't got any money.

V
1. What did you buy?

2. How long are you going for?

3. What's your favourite subject?

4. How did they get there?

5. Did it rain yesterday?

6. Why did she laugh?

VI
1. I will go swimming next Saturday.

2. My cousin loves swimming.

3. There's a swimming pool on Wood Road.

4. I'm going to a water park next Saturday.

5. We can get the bus.

6. I will meet you at the bus stop.

7. The park is near the supermarket.

8. My friend Paul is coming too.

Week 3 每周一练

I 　1. in 　　　2. on 　　　3. at 　　　4. at 　　　5. in 　　　6. at

II 　1. because 　2. but 　　3. so 　　　4. because 　5. so 　　　6. but

III 　1. F 　　　2. E 　　　3. B 　　　4. C 　　　5. D 　　　6. A

IV 　1. We can't wear jeans to school.

　2. I would love to stay out late tonight.

　3. We can meet at six o'clock beside the town clock.

　4. Sorry I couldn't go to the concert yesterday.

　5. You should take some food.

　6. Do you have to go to school on weekends?

　7. I will arrive at the train station on Monday afternoon.

　8. I am going to stay with an English friend next week.

V 　1. Was he late?

　2. What are you doing?

　3. Are you going to Dave's party?

　4. Where are you going to stay?

　5. How often do you go swimming?

　6. What kind of music do you like?

VI 　1. What about meeting at the station?

　2. I'm very pleased you will go with me.

　3. I'm afraid that I can't come.

　4. It's great that you are free on Sunday.

　5. Can we go on Friday instead?

　6. Let's meet at the subway station.

　7. Why don't we take the bus together?

　8. Don't forget to wear comfortable clothes.

Week 4 每周一练

I 　1. on 　　　2. in 　　　3. at 　　　4. in 　　　5. in 　　　6. on

II 1. watched   2. violin   3. late   4. receive   5. promise   6. afraid

III 1. D   2. A   3. C   4. F   5. E   6. B

IV 1. She is always happy!

2. My sister plays the piano once a week.

3. I often visit my grandmother at the weekend.

4. My mother drives to work every day.

5. I usually have breakfast at 7 a.m.

6. I sometimes watch TV in the evening.

7. I go to the gym three times a week.

8. I will never forget your kindness.

V 1. When will you arrive?

2. Did they enjoy the party?

3. Where did he go?

4. When can we meet?

5. Who did you speak to?

6. How much homework do you get every day?

VI 1. I'm afraid I can't come to your party!

2. I'm sorry, but I'll be a bit late.

3. I'm going to see a movie this Saturday.

4. Would you like to come with me?

5. Shall we go to the cinema tomorrow evening?

6. Do you want to come too?

7. How about we meet at the subway station?

8. Let's meet near the supermarket.

Week 5 每周一练

I 1. was   2. did   3. went   4. called   5. came   6. looked

7. made   8. put   9. ran   10. said   11. saw   12. told

II 1. because   2. but   3. but   4. so   5. and   6. but

7. so   8. because

III　1. watched　　2. ran　　　3. shouted　　4. made　　　5. played　　6. relaxed

IV　1. F　　　　2. A　　　　3. B　　　　4. C　　　　5. D　　　　6. E

V　1. × have改为had　　　　　　2. × go改为went

　　3. × homeworks改为homework　　4. √

　　5. × chocolates改为chocolate　　6. √

VI　1. He had two tickets for the new film which starts at 10:30.

　　2. They were talking about a film that they watched yesterday.

　　3. They saw a girl who was holding a map.

　　4. She saw some black shoes which she liked.

　　5. Ketty saw a girl who looked scared.

　　6. He spoke to a waiter who worked in the restaurant.

　　7. She took off the coat which she was wearing.

　　8. The old woman was carrying a bag which looked heavy.

Week 6 每周一练

I　1. enjoyed　　2. entered　　3. flew　　　4. got　　　5. gave　　　6. kept

　7. paid　　　8. sent　　　9. took　　　10. walked　11. washed　12. won

II　1. eggs　　　2. bread　　　3. water　　　4. any　　　5. milk　　　6. chocolate

　7. money　　8. a

III　1. called　　2. threw　　　3. had　　　4. jumped　　5. ate　　　6. sang

IV　1. E　　　　2. C　　　　3. B　　　　4. F　　　　5. A　　　　6. D

V　1. × doesn't改为didn't　　　　2. √

　　3. × starts改为started　　　　4. × quiet改为quietly

　　5. × waters改为water　　　　6. √

VI　1. He didn't look at his clock.

　　2. The weather was great at the weekend.

　　3. It was warm and sunny. / It was sunny and warm.

　　4. I heard the thunderstorm last night.

　　5. Max was in the city centre with his mum.

　　6. He decided to play football.

7. Martin decided to make a cake.

8. She went to the supermarket to buy some eggs.

Week 7 每周一练

I   1. were   2. arrived   3. brought   4. collected   5. decided   6. built

       7. heard   8. jumped   9. played   10. turned   11. visited   12. watched

II   1. new   2. happy   3. polite   4. busy   5. interested   6. great

       7. small   8. wonderful

III   1. raining   2. watching   3. run   4. eaten   5. listening   6. lived

IV   1. B   2. A   3. D   4. C   5. F   6. E

V   1. × visit改为visited   2. × slow改为slowly

       3. × quick改为quickly   4. × are改为is

       5. × room改为rooms   6. √

VI   1. When he cycled in the park, he saw Alice.

       2. It was John's birthday, so he and his parents went to his favourite restaurant.

       3. David wasn't late because his mum gave him a lift.

       4. They were all very hungry, so they ordered two pizzas on the menu.

       5. I put my pen back in my bag after I found it.

       6. When I was fishing yesterday, I met a really interesting person.

       7. He was happy because it was a sunny day.

       8. After Bob arrived at the park, he saw that many people were already there.

附录

可数名词复数变化规则

可数名词复数的规则变化				
序号	词尾	变化公式	举个例子	
1	——	词尾+s	手 hand	手 hands
2	-ch、-sh、-s、-x	词尾+es	班级 class 狐狸 fox	班级 classes 狐狸 foxes
3	辅音字母+y	y → ies	家庭 family	家庭 families
4	元音字母+y	词尾+s	玩具 toy	玩具 toys
5	辅音字母+o (有生命)	词尾+es	土豆 potato	土豆 potatoes
6	元音字母+o (无生命)	词尾+s	录像 video	录像 videos
7	-f、-fe	f / fe → ves	刀子 knife	刀子 knives

可数名词复数的不规则变化				
序号	变化公式	举个例子		
1	oo变ee	脚 foot 脚 feet	牙齿 tooth 牙齿 teeth	鹅 goose 鹅 geese
2	不变	绵羊 sheep	鱼 fish	鹿 deer
3	其他特殊变化	男人 man 男人 men	孩子 child 孩子 children	老鼠 mouse 老鼠 mice

A2 Key不规则动词表

1. 改变元音字母

序号	变形规律	动词原形	过去式	中文释义
1	i变为a	begin	began	开始
		drink	drank	喝
		give	gave	给；交给；送给
		ring	rang	响铃；按铃；给……打电话

序号	变形规律	动词原形	过去式	中文释义
1	i变为a	sing	sang	唱歌
		sit	sat	坐
		spit	spat	吐（唾沫、食物等）；怒斥
		swim	swam	游泳
2	o变为a	become	became	变得；成为
		come	came	来；出现
3	a变为o	wake	woke	叫醒；醒来
4	i变为o	drive	drove	驾驶
		ride	rode	骑马；乘车
		shine	shone	闪光；闪耀
		win	won	赢得，获胜
		write	wrote	写
5	e变为o	forget	forgot	忘记
		get	got	成为；获得；到达
6	o变为e	hold	held	拿着，抓住；举行
7	ow / aw变为ew	blow	blew	吹
		draw	drew	画；拉
		grow	grew	生长；种植
		know	knew	知道；了解
		throw	threw	投，扔，抛
8	其他变化	dig	dug	挖
		fall	fell	落下；跌倒
		hang	hung	悬挂，吊
		run	ran	跑
9	省略相同字母中的一个	choose	chose	选择
		feed	fed	喂养；进食
		meet	met	遇见；集合；开会
		shoot	shot	射击；射杀
10	去掉单词结尾的e	bite	bit	咬
		hide	hid	隐藏；躲避

2. 改变辅音（元音＋辅音）字母

序号	变形规律	动词原形	过去式	中文释义
1	省略两个相同字母中的一个，词尾加t	feel	felt	感觉
		keep	kept	保持；继续；留着；养；饲养
		sleep	slept	睡觉
		sweep	swept	打扫
		smell	smelt	闻
2	在动词原形后加一个辅音字母d或t	burn	burnt / burned	燃烧；灼伤
		dream	dreamt / dreamed	做梦；梦想
		hear	heard	听见；听说
		learn	learnt / learned	学习；获悉；了解
		mean	meant	意味着；意思是；打算
3	把动词原形的最后一个辅音字母d变为t	build	built	建造
		send	sent	发送；派遣；寄信
		spend	spent	度过；花费
4	k变为d	make	made	使，让；做，制造；整理（床铺等）
5	y变为id	pay	paid	支付；给以报酬
		say	said	说，讲

3. 过去式包含ought、aught

序号	变形规律	动词原形	过去式	中文释义
1	过去式包含ought	bring	brought	带来
		buy	bought	购买
		think	thought	想，思考；认为，以为
		seek	sought	寻找；搜寻
2	过去式包含aught	catch	caught	抓住；赶上
		teach	taught	教学

4. 过去式和动词原形一样

序号	变形规律	动词原形	过去式	中文释义
1	过去式和动词原形一样	bet	bet	打赌
		cost	cost	花费
		cut	cut	切，割
		hit	hit	打，打击
		hurt	hurt	伤害
		let	let	让，允许
		put	put	放；安置
		read	read（读音发生改变）	阅读；朗读
		shut	shut	关闭；关上
		spread	spread	展开；传播；散布

5. 情态动词的特殊变形

序号	动词原形	过去式	中文释义
1	can	could	能，会；可以；可能
2	may	might	可能，也许；可以
3	must	must	必须；一定
4	shall	should	将要
5	will	would	将，将要

6. 其他不规则变形

序号	变形规律	动词原形	过去式	中文释义
1	ear变为ore	bear	bore	忍受
		wear	wore	穿（衣服、鞋），戴；损耗
2	eak变为oke	break	broke	打破，破碎；损坏
		speak	spoke	讲话；发言；讲述
3	ell变为old	sell	sold	出售；转让；推销
		tell	told	告诉；讲述

续表

序号	变形规律	动词原形	过去式	中文释义
4	ake变为ook	shake	shook	摇动；摇头；握手
		take	took	拿；采取；花费
5	无规律变化	eat	ate	吃
		find	found	找到；发现
		go	went	去，走
		have	had	有；做；进行；从事
		leave	left	离开；留下
		lie	lay（躺）lied（说谎）	说谎；躺
		lose	lost	丢失；丧失
		see	saw	看见，看出；观看
		stand	stood	站立；起立
		steal	stole	偷，窃取

小马外语